Finding Jobs
With a
Psychology Bachelor's Degree

Finding Jobs

With a

Psychology Bachelor's Degree

Expert Advice for Launching Your Career

R. Eric Landrum

AMERICAN PSYCHOLOGICAL ASSOCIATION
Washington, DC

Published by
American Psychological Association
750 First Street, NE
Washington, DC 20002
www.apa.org

To order
APA Order Department
P.O. Box 92984
Washington, DC 20090-2984
Tel: (800) 374-2721; Direct: (202) 336-5510
Fax: (202) 336-5502; TDD/TTY: (202) 336-6123
Online: www.apa.org/books/
E-mail: order@apa.org

In the U.K., Europe, Africa, and the Middle East, copies may be ordered from
American Psychological Association
3 Henrietta Street
Covent Garden, London
WC2E 8LU England

Typeset in Meridian by Circle Graphics, Columbia, MD

Printer: Gasch Printing, Odenton, MD
Cover Designer: Mercury Publishing Services, Rockville, MD
Technical/Production Editor: Dan Brachtesende

The opinions and statements published are the responsibility of the authors, and such opinions and statements do not necessarily represent the policies of the American Psychological Association.

Library of Congress Cataloging-in-Publication Data

Landrum, R. Eric.
  Finding jobs with a psychology bachelor's degree : expert advice for launching your career /
R. Eric Landrum. — 1st ed.
    p. cm.
  Includes bibliographical references (p.) and index.
  ISBN-13: 978-1-4338-0437-3
  ISBN-10: 1-4338-0437-9
  1. Psychology—Vocational guidance. I. Title.

  BF76.L35 2009
  150.23—dc22   2008041449

British Library Cataloguing-in-Publication Data
A CIP record is available from the British Library.

Printed in the United States of America
First Edition

10 9 8 7 6 5 4 3

*Dedicated to undergraduate psychology majors
and to Allison and Scott.*

Contents

IV

Preface: From Bachelor's Degree to Career Success

The ultimate goal of attending college is to leave college—with a degree, one hopes, but more than that, with a degree and a host of experiences that have prepared you for a lifetime of learning and of educated citizenry and to be a productive and fulfilled member of the workforce. I've written this book to fill a void: If you are a psychology major (or someone who advises psychology majors), you know that many of your student colleagues are interested in graduate school—and maybe you are, too. Most of the postbaccalaureate attention that psychology majors receive is about what you can do if you go on to graduate school in psychology. There are many books and resources about entry into graduate school. However, if you are like the majority of undergraduate psychology majors, you won't attend graduate school, and you're seeking meaningful employment in the workforce. This book is for you.

Because there are so few resources available specifically for psychology majors entering the workforce, I started by collecting some data. Through an arduous process that I describe in chapter 11, I contacted (with the help of talented research assistants) individuals from across the country in the workforce with only a bachelor's degree in psychology. These individuals graciously completed an online interview, and their responses make up much of this book. You'll get to read, in their own words, about their experiences as a psychology major while an undergraduate and how these experiences connected to their future employment, sometimes directly and sometimes by a more circuitous route. You should know, however, that the survey responses are the opinions of the responders; I did not edit those comments for

---

Employer information in surveys (see chaps. 3–6) is listed as provided by survey participants and is not necessarily accurate or up to date.

accuracy. As you read the interviews, organized by Holland Codes (see chap. 2), themes emerge that I emphasize in chapter 7. However, the helpfulness of this book does not end there.

After you have read the interviews and thought about the emerging themes, you'll encounter a trio of chapters designed to help you jump-start the process of finding a great job with your bachelor's degree in psychology. You'll read about tips for the job-hunting process, writing a cover letter, crafting your résumé, and what to do and not to do during an interview. This is practical advice on how to reach your goals. The interviews give you a sense of what you can achieve with your undergraduate degree; the practical advice chapters provide a road map of how to get from where you are now to a successful position in the workforce.

Books like this one do not pop out of nowhere. I sincerely appreciate the advice and support of Linda Malnasi McCarter, acquisitions editor in the American Psychological Association (APA) Books Department, who saw value in this project from the very beginning and was so patient during the revision process. I thank Linda (again) for her vote of confidence in me, and I also support Linda's philosophy of providing invaluable resources for undergraduate psychology students. Another key person to thank is Susan Herman, development editor at APA Books. Susan provided insightful advice about improving every aspect of the book you are now reading. She has this wonderful ability to see potential—to see what is currently on the page and to imagine what it can be. The third member of my publishing "dream team" is Dan Brachtesende, production supervisor at APA Books. His attention to detail made this entire book better. Let me assure you that I am fully responsible for the final product you hold here, but any success that this book experiences owes a debt to Linda, Susan, and Dan. I thank them all for their efforts.

It is my sincere hope that the ideas in the book will help you better understand what you can do with your bachelor's degree in psychology and will give you some tips on how to launch into that process of finding your success. If you can think of anything that I can do to help, please e-mail me at ericlandrum@msn.com. Your suggestions are both welcome and valuable, and in future editions of this book I will add more resources to improve this advice to undergraduate psychology students and their advisors.

MAKING YOURSELF WORKFORCE READY

What Is Career Success to You?
An Inventory of Expectations

1

Collect is great! I mean it. It really is. You have a good amount of structure provided for you. You're told when to be at what building for this lecture or that activity. You're given detailed instructions on how tasks are to be completed and definite timelines and multiple opportunities for help. If you live on campus, you probably have a meal plan, and someone cooks for you every day. If you live off campus, well then, you get to enjoy living off campus! If you've already been in the workforce, you know how different college is from the "real world." College has many wonderful aspects. But if you are doing your work, and the faculty are doing their work, college is designed to eventually come to an end (unless you never want to leave, and in that case you become a professor!)

At some point during your undergraduate career, you'll need to start thinking about your future. Not in some hypothetical, abstract way, but realistically: What are you going to do after you receive your bachelor's degree in psychology? Some graduates go on to graduate school in psychology or law school or medical school, but the majority of students receiving a bachelor's degree in psychology do not pursue further education. So the question becomes this: How do you launch your career with a bachelor's degree in psychology?

The purpose of this book is to present psychology majors (and those who advise them) with a series of profiles of people in careers that were achieved with a bachelor's degree in psychology. After presenting the profiles, I provide concrete advice about how to launch the next phase of your career. My goal is for you to better understand various career options by gaining a real-world perspective from folks currently in a particular field. This approach also emphasizes the diversity of opportunity within psychology and emphasizes the value of the knowledge, skills, and abilities earned at the undergraduate level—not from a professor's perspective but from the words and inspiration of other recipients of bachelor's degrees in psychology. O'Hara (2005) stated, "the best way to learn about how to find a job and the various types of ways you can use a psychology degree is to listen to and read about real stories, real people, and real experiences" (p. 71). I cannot say whether this is the best way or not, but I think presenting this information in a person's own words, in narrative form, is very powerful. That is why I wrote this book.

What You Want in a Job or Career

In the past 14 years, more than 1 million undergraduate students received their bachelor's degrees in psychology (Snyder, Dillow, & Hoffman, 2008). The number of students interested in psychology continues to soar, as evidenced by the ever-increasing number of psychology bachelor's degrees awarded each year. The most recent data available from the National Center for Education Statistics (Snyder et al., 2008) revealed that in 2005–2006 there were 88,134 bachelor's degrees awarded in psychology. Although the estimates vary, somewhere around 20% to 25% of these students end up continuing their education through graduate school in psychology (Landrum, Klein, Horan, & Wynn, 2008). However, this means that the majority of psychology bachelor's degree recipients do not attend graduate school, but have an interest in obtaining a good job with their bachelor's degree. This book is for this majority of students; by listening to those with the most credibility—other successful bachelor's degree holders—current students can learn what leads to success and how to prepare for that success while still an undergraduate.

Tip: Because of the high numbers of psychology graduates, competition for psychology-related jobs is keen. Getting good grades may not be enough to guarantee that you will find satisfying work after college.

You'll see from the profiles presented in chapters 3 through 6 that grades are rarely mentioned; it's the skills and abilities learned along the way—along with a positive work ethic—that gets you hired and keeps you employed.

Although the bulk of those with a psychology baccalaureate do not pursue further education, there are relatively few resources (or research) for psychology baccalaureates compared with those available for graduate students. This book is intended to help fill that void. To my knowledge, there is nothing out there that does what this book does—presents multiple profiles of successful individuals with a bachelor's degree in psychology in those individuals' own words. Couple that first-hand information with concrete advice for job seeking, and you have in hand a powerful tool to launch your future career.

> Tip: You don't have to have a master's degree or doctoral degree in psychology to find satisfying work that is relevant to the psychology major.

That is not to say that there isn't any information available about careers for those with a bachelor's degree in psychology; there are some very good resources. Books such as *Opportunities in Psychology Careers* (Super & Super, 1995) and *Great Jobs for Psychology Majors* (DeGalan & Lambert, 2006) offer general advice about the discipline of psychology and the job search process and provide some information about career paths. *Great Jobs for Psychology Majors,* for example, presents five career paths: residential care, social and human services, human resources, therapy, and teaching (DeGalan & Lambert, 2006). Two of my favorite books that discuss career options for psychology baccalaureates are *Majoring in Psych? Career Options for Psychology Undergraduates* (Morgan & Korschgen, 2009) and *The Psychology Major: Career Options and Strategies for Success* (Landrum & Davis, 2007). *Majoring in Psych?* is a great, quick read that provides career information and also addresses graduate school decisions and choices. *The Psychology Major* includes information about bachelor's degree options and how to pursue them. However, neither of these presents detailed narratives about actual psychology graduates. The closest example comes from *What Can You Do With a Major in Psychology?* (O'Hara, 2005). This book provides six case studies: an art therapist, sports psychologist, forensic psychologist, corporate psychologist, community psychologist, and school psychologist. However, five of these six case studies are about individuals who continued their education beyond the bachelor's degree.

There are also numerous resources available in print and on the Internet that provide job-seeking advice, résumé preparation, how to write a cover letter, tips for interviewing, and so forth. However, in this one resource I provide a brief overview on how to successfully complete these important tasks.

Other works present career path information as well. For example, there are numerous profiles of career paths for psychologists; however, they seem to be exclusive to doctoral-level psychologists and perhaps not as relevant to psychology baccalaureates. For example, *Career Paths in Psychology: Where Your Degree Can Take You* (Sternberg, 1997) provides valuable information about different career paths, but it focuses on graduate-level (doctoral) degrees, not on what an undergraduate can achieve with the bachelor's degree in psychology. In a wonderful article on career paths ("The Career Path Less Traveled," 2001), the American Psychological Association (APA) published a series of 21 vignettes on those with off-the-beaten-path careers. However, of these 21 individuals, 20 had a PhD in psychology and 1 had a PsyD.

What does this all mean? There are numerous guides available to students that can provide some valuable information about careers in psychology (Kuther & Morgan, 2007; Landrum & Davis, 2007; Morgan & Korschgen, 2009; Super & Super, 1995). There are also some resources available that present multiple career paths (DeGalan & Lambert, 2006; O'Hara, 2005; Sternberg, 1997). However, there appears to be no resource available that provides multiple examples of what you can do with a bachelor's degree in psychology in the voices of those living such a success story.

Such stories are told here, in each person's own words, starting in chapter 3. Although that is the main goal of this book, I have other goals too, such as hands-on career preparation advice and tips. I want to provide you with as much useful information as I can in the space provided—in other words, to give you the most bang for your buck. If you are reading this, you will probably be pursuing a job with your bachelor's degree in psychology soon, or you advise and mentor those pursuing a psychology baccalaureate. Although you are still an undergraduate, you have time to make adjustments before you graduate so that you can fully maximize your undergraduate experience. In the remaining portions of this chapter, I present some information about six important topics: (a) what employers want from psychology baccalaureates, (b) what APA wants from psychology baccalaureates, (c) advantages of a liberal arts education, (d) transitioning from college to career, (e) stages of career development, and (f) predictors of career satisfaction. I believe that if you have some information about these topics before graduation, it will allow you to maximize your opportunities while you are still an undergraduate. If you are a student reading this book, what might you be looking for? First, I want you to see the variety of jobs, careers, and occupational settings that your bachelor's degree in psychology prepares you for. You'll see that you are not "typecast" at all, and that your skills and abilities, if properly developed as an undergraduate and honed as an employee, will carry you far. Second, I want you to have a realistic preview of what the job market may be like for you. Like many, many job sectors, you'll probably start at the bottom and need to work your way up. This book will give you a realistic preview, with salaries, workload issues, etc. Third, you should be looking for postbaccalaureate opportunities that challenge you and allow you to grow. I know it sounds odd to want more challenges just after you've finished college, but most people thrive on challenge and need to continue after college. Mastering these challenges helps you to gain confidence as well as acquire new skills and abilities that will make you more marketable and more valuable to your employer. As you will read, many people go far with their bachelor's degree in psychology—odds are, you can too.

What Employers Want From Psychology Baccalaureates

There have been numerous efforts to identify what skills are most desirable in psychology graduates. For example, employers of psychology graduates were asked to rate the most important of 88 different skills and abilities (Landrum & Harrold, 2003). The top 10 abilities, starting with the most important, are (a) listening skills; (b) ability to work with others as part of a team; (c) getting along with others; (d) desire and willingness to learn; (e) willingness to learn new, important skills; (f) focus on customers or clients; (g) interpersonal relationship skills; (h) adaptability to changing situations; (i) ability to suggest solutions to problems; and (j) problem-solving skills. As you read through the narratives in this book, you can verify for yourself the importance of these skills and abilities. Also note that although you can learn some of these in school, others are traits you already possess but can practice and sharpen while in school.

In a separate study, 39 employers of psychology majors completed a survey (Appleby, 2000). These employers were asked to sort specific skills groups into categories. The results indicated five major categories of job skills: (a) social skills (e.g., deals effectively with a wide variety of people); (b) personal skills (e.g., shows initiative and persistence, effective time management); (c) communication skills (e.g., listens carefully and accurately); (d) information-gathering and information-processing skills (e.g., plans and carries out projects successfully, thinks logically and creatively); and (e) numerical, computer, and psychometric skills (e.g., displays computer literacy). Odds are you are already strong in some of these areas; you should take courses and seek out experiences that keep these strengths strong. Additionally, and this is not often popular advice, you should also seek out opportunities and experiences to improve your weaknesses. Thus, if you are absolutely fearful of writing or math, I suggest that you confront those weaknesses and take more classes in those areas, as opposed to avoiding what you are not good at. It's difficult to get good at something if you never practice it.

Tip: Certain skills you need for the workplace (e.g., work ethic, desire to learn) you will have to develop independently of your academic program.

A survey of employers who hire psychology graduates also reported some negative outcomes of recent hires (Appleby, 2000). Employers had observed that recently hired psychology graduates (a) had a poor work ethic (i.e., complaints about having to work hard to obtain what they wanted), (b) were too dependent on textbook knowledge, (c) believed that they were overqualified, and (d) were searching for their next job rather than mastering the one they had. Generally speaking (not just pertaining to psychology majors), more recent research has identified the top six reasons that new hires are fired (Gardner, 2007): (a) unethical behavior, (b) lack of motivation or work ethic, (c) inappropriate use of technology, (d) failure to follow instructions, (e) being late for work, and (f) missing assignment deadlines. Look at these reasons why new hires get fired: You can practice avoiding these behaviors (and thus maximize future opportunities) while you are still in college. By following instructions and getting assignments in on time, you are practicing skills for your future. By getting to class on time, you are practicing getting to work on time. Thus, faculty members who penalize late work or penalize you for missing class are actually attempting to mold your behavior for the future. Psychology also places a high degree of emphasis on ethical behavior, which bodes well for your future as a new hire and keeping your job.

What APA Wants From Psychology Baccalaureates

Employers are not the only ones who have expectations for psychology graduates. A task force working with APA identified 10 undergraduate psychology learning goals and outcomes that are of such importance that I present them here (see Exhibit 1.1). They are divided into five goals that address the knowledge, skills, and values consistent with the science and application of psychology and five goals that focus on the knowledge, skills, and values consistent with a liberal arts education (it is hoped that psychology courses also further accomplishments in these areas; American Psychological Association, 2007).

This book is particularly helpful in nurturing the items on the second portion of the list. In particular, by reading the profiles of other psychology baccalaureates, you can enhance your sociocultural awareness

---

EXHIBIT 1.1

Undergraduate Psychology Major Competencies

Knowledge, skills, and values consistent with the science and application of psychology
  1. Knowledge base of psychology—Students will demonstrate familiarity with the major concepts, theoretical perspectives, empirical findings, and historical trends in psychology.
  2. Research methods in psychology—Students will understand and apply basic research methods in psychology, including research design, data analysis, and interpretation.
  3. Critical thinking skills in psychology—Students will respect and use critical and creative thinking, skeptical inquiry, and, when possible, the scientific approach to solve problems related to behavior and mental processes.
  4. Application of psychology—Students will understand and apply psychological principles to personal, social, and organizational issues.
  5. Values in psychology—Students will be able to weigh evidence, tolerate ambiguity, act ethically, and reflect other values that are the underpinnings of psychology as a discipline.

Knowledge, skills, and values consistent with liberal arts education that are further developed in psychology
  6. Information and technological literacy—Students will demonstrate information competence and the ability to use computers and other technology for many purposes.
  7. Communication skills—Students will be able to communicate effectively in a variety of formats.
  8. Sociocultural and international awareness—Students will recognize, understand, and respect the complexity of sociocultural and international diversity.
  9. Personal development—Students will develop insight into their own and others' behavior and mental process and apply effective strategies for self-management and self-improvement.
  10. Career planning and development—Students will emerge from the major with realistic ideas about how to implement their psychological knowledge, skills, and values in occupational pursuits in a variety of settings.

(No. 8) and gain insight into personal development (No. 9) by reading about others' personal development. Finally, this book should help tremendously in achieving Goal Number 10: It provides real examples of psychology graduates who are successful in a number of different occupations and careers, and it provides resources to help you successfully transition from your undergraduate experience into the workplace.

The Advantage of a Liberal Arts Education

You'll probably have about eight different jobs that may span three different professions or occupations (Chen, 2004). Knowing this, how can you prepare for all of these different work environments and situations? Well, you can and you can't. That is, you can't anticipate every twist and turn your life will take. You won't be able to prepare for every contingency for every type of career, even for all those careers you may sincerely be interested in.

In another way, though, you can prepare yourself, generally speaking, for the multiple careers you will likely encounter. It's called a liberal arts education. What does that mean?

> One of the major characteristics of a "liberal" or "liberal arts" education is that it is not focused on a specific career, but aims instead to provide an environment both within the curriculum and outside it that helps students to learn how to think, how to be creative, how to be flexible, how to get on with others— and how to go on learning for the rest of their lives. (Chen, 2004, p. 2)

Some of the goals of an undergraduate education are even larger. All universities attempt to produce better educated citizens who are capable of using higher order critical thinking skills. I believe that if you exit your undergraduate experience with a love of learning, then you will be well on your way to success, and not just career success.

These ideas are not just my own, but have been articulated by others well before me (and much more eloquently). John Henry Newman (1852/1960, pp. 177–178) expressed these sentiments long ago in his treatise "The Idea of a University":

> If then a practical end must be assigned to a University course, I say it is that of training good members of society. Its art is the art of social life, and its end is fitness for the world. It neither confines its views to particular professions on one hand, nor creates heroes or inspires genius on the other. Works indeed of genius fall under no art; heroic minds come under no rule; a University is not a birthplace of poets or of immortal authors, of founders of schools, leaders of colonies, or conquerors of nations. It does not promise a generation of Aristotles or Newtons, of Napoleons or Washingtons, of Raphaels or Shakespeares, though such miracles it has before now contained within its precincts. Nor is it content on the other hand with forming the critic or the experimentalist, the economist or the engineer, although such too it includes within its scope. But a university training is the great ordinary means to a great but ordinary end; it aims at raising the intellectual tone of society, at cultivating the public mind, at purifying the national taste, at supplying true principles to popular enthusiasm and fixed aims to popular aspiration, at giving enlargement and sobriety to the ideas of the age, at facilitating the exercise of political power, and refining the intercourse of private life. It is the education which gives a [person] a clear, conscious view of their own opinions and judgements, a truth in developing them, an eloquence in expressing them, and a force in urging them.

After Graduation: Transitioning From College to Career

For some time now, my colleague Paul Hettich has been studying college students and how they make a successful transition to careers in the workforce (Hettich, 1998; Hettich & Helkowski, 2005). He has written extensively on the topic, and not only has he clearly identified the issues, but he has also offered tips on how to make the transition smoothly and successfully. To see how challenging the transition can be on multiple levels, see Exhibit 1.2.

So how do you deal with all of these transitional issues? Hettich (2004) provided some concrete suggestions as to how to make the transition smoothly:

■ Complete courses that focus directly on specific organizational aspects of the workplace, such as management, leadership,

---

EXHIBIT 1.2

Graduates' Perceived Differences Between College and Workplace

College	Workplace
Frequent and concrete feedback	Infrequent, nonspecific feedback
Some freedom to set a schedule	Less freedom or control over schedule
Frequent breaks and time off	Limited time off
Choose performance level	A-level work expected continuously
Correct answers usually available	Few right answers
Passive participation permitted	Active participation and initiative expected
Independent thinking supported	Independent thinking often discouraged
Environment of personal support	Usually less personal support
Focus on personal development	Focus on getting results for organization
Structured courses and curriculum	Much less structure, fewer directions
Few changes in routine	Often constant and unexpected changes
Personal control over time	Responds to supervisor's directions
Individual effort and performance	Often, team effort and performance
Intellectual challenge	Organizational and people challenges
Acquisition of knowledge	Acquisition and application of knowledge
Professors	Supervisors

Note. From "From College to Corporate Culture: You're a Freshman Again," by J. Hettich, 2004, presented at the Midwestern Psychological Association meeting, Chicago; from "Preparing Students for Life Beyond the Classroom" by E. F. Holton III, in *The Senior Year Experience: Facilitating Integration, Reflection, Closure, and Transition,* by J. N. Gardner & G. Van der Veer (Eds.), 1998, San Francisco: Jossey-Bass. Copyright 1998 by Jossey-Bass. Adapted with permission.

communication and group skills, organizational behavior, the sociology of organizations, career planning, and human resources.

- Enroll in workshops, seminars, or courses that focus on self-development, leadership, conflict management, team building, interpersonal communication, time management, stress management, and similar professional skills.
- Join clubs, sports, and campus organizations in which collaboration, teamwork, conflict, communication, and leadership are practiced as constructive tools.
- Complete internships and perform volunteer work.
- Collect evidence of curricular and cocurricular achievements, including papers, projects, awards, and performance evaluations, and organize them in an electronic portfolio that monitors personal progress and serves as a tool in job searches.
- Recognize that grades, test scores, and GPAs are often skewed predictors of intelligence in the workplace.
- Remember that teachers cannot give students all the answers because they don't know all the answers, just some of them.

What is fascinating here is that almost all of the points that Hettich (2004) made are also mentioned in the interviews presented in this book. The results of these interviews demonstrate quite clearly that you are employable with a bachelor's degree in psychology. However, I also like this blunt summarization of the relationship between selecting your major and getting a good job: "No matter what you major in, if you can't answer the phone, make a presentation, do a spreadsheet, or write a business letter, nobody needs you" (Combs, 2000, p. 14).

Stages of Career Development

There are numerous theories of career development, and this section is not meant as a comprehensive review of those theories. Rather, I summarize this particular career development stage model to highlight that your career will not be one unitary, stagnant "thing." It will shift, evolve, change, and adapt in a series of stages. I think it is useful to think about these stages because it also highlights the fact that your education and training will not be complete after you receive your bachelor's degree in psychology. Almost all of the interviewees mention continued training and workshops after college. I hope by now you also realize (and believe) that education is the key to the future. Think about the stages of career development described below and how you might be able to make smooth transitions in your career as you ebb and flow through these stages (Driver, 1988, cited in Wahlstrom & Williams, 2004).

STAGE 1: DECIDING ON YOUR CAREER

Ideally, the time to explore career options would be during college. Perhaps you decided to attend college with a clear career goal in mind; you may still have that career goal, or you may have changed your mind. It's okay to change your mind, but eventually you want to settle on something so you can graduate (I actually went to college to major in math, changed to business, added speech communication and theater arts, and then added psychology, eventually double majoring in the last two). College is a great time to explore different majors and their related career paths.

STAGE 2: PREPARING FOR YOUR CAREER

Once you have some tentative ideas about a career path, then it's time to start gathering information. Talk with as many people as you can to gain more information. Try to find someone who has your perfect job and get to know them, perhaps even interview them. Ideally, in your career preparation in college you can complete an internship or some other outside-of-class experience. An internship is a great hands-on way to explore a career path without fully committing to that path. Your coursework, your assignments, and the skills and abilities you gain through your classes also provide you with essential career preparation.

STAGE 3: FINDING AN ENTRY-LEVEL POSITION

You may be able to find that entry-level position while still in college, perhaps as an internship. But almost everyone starts at the bottom rung of the ladder and works up from there. During these work experiences, it is essential that you hone your job skills, but also skills such as writing an effective résumé, developing self-confidence and interviewing skills, and so forth. Numerous books and resources can help with this, and some are specifically designed for psychology majors (e.g., Landrum & Davis, 2007). The later chapters of this book also provide advice in many of these areas.

STAGE 4: LEARNING THE JOB, SHOWING YOUR STUFF, AND FINDING MENTORS

During this early career stage, you are showing that you know what to do to be successful, and you are also willing to work hard to achieve that success. Not only are you learning the job, but you are also learning how to be successful in the career by understanding and following the written and unwritten rules. By helping your company or organization achieve its goals, you demonstrate your worth and value. During this career stage, you demonstrate that you have indeed made the transition from college to career, and you are ramping up for the most productive stage of your career. During this stage, effective mentoring is critical and can make a major difference in your career trajectory (Driver, 1988). An effective mentor can help you navigate the sometimes tricky waters of the business world and can be an essential networking resource.

STAGE 5: YOUR MIDCAREER: ERA OF MAJOR ACCOMPLISHMENTS

During this stage, which could last 20 to 35 years (Driver, 1988), you are at the height of your career, and you achieve the most. By this stage, you have solid training and experience to succeed and excel at your job. Depending on your career path, you may be moving up in your organization or looking for opportunities in other organizations for personal and professional advancement. You may face obstacles along the way, such as hitting a glass ceiling or finding that you have achieved all you can in a certain career with a particular organization.

STAGE 6: YOUR LATE CAREER

At some point in most careers, people level out or reach a plateau in the career advancement sequence; this may be the time you begin to think about retirement or to refocus and seek out new challenges. This could possibly be the most enjoyable portion of your career path—you are established, you have an impressive skill set, you have worked long enough to be self-confident, and you have acquired wisdom along the way. With the most productive push of your career behind you, you can think more about the big picture, whether that is in the context of your organization or your own personal career.

As an undergraduate, you can start to build toward your future career. You should start a résumé. You should participate in activities that not only help you build a strong résumé, but also help you build mentoring relationships that can lead to professional references or letters of recommendation. You should also take classes and participate in class projects that help build the interpersonal skills that will lead to success in interviews. What do I mean by interpersonal skills? Yancey, Clarkson, Baxa, and Clarkson (2003) articulated a cogent list of interpersonal competencies: (a) effectively translating and conveying information, (b) being able to accurately interpret other people's emotions, (c) being sensitive to other people's feelings, (d) calmly arriving at resolutions to conflict, (e) avoiding gossip, and (f) being polite. Focus on these interpersonal skills while you are an undergraduate, and you'll be well on your way to success.

Predictors of Career Satisfaction

This book is all about providing you with real examples of people with successful careers with their bachelor's degree in psychology. It is true that each of us has to define success for ourselves, but there is a body of valuable research that helps us to understand career satisfaction and, perhaps more important, the predictors of career satisfaction. The information available is sometimes generalized across disciplines and careers, and sometimes this information is focused just on careers emerging with a bachelor's degree in psychology.

In a recent section of the General Social Survey, more than 27,000 Americans were surveyed about job satisfaction and job happiness (Smith, 2007). According to this survey, "the most satisfying jobs are most professions, especially those involving caring for, teaching, and protecting others and creative pursuits" (p. 1); with regard to happiness, "most of the occupations ranking high in general happiness are professions involving helping others, technical and scientific expertise, or creativity" (p. 2). Of course, only you will be able to determine what works for you, but with your bachelor's degree in psychology, it is more than likely that you will be helping others, by helping change behavior, helping through business ventures, helping through sales, and so forth. Those in careers and professions that involve helping others do quite well with respect to satisfaction and happiness (Smith, 2007).

Although the general information about career satisfaction and happiness is interesting, there are also specific data available about psychology majors and the careers they pursue with a bachelor's degree. Much of this literature focuses on the information that advisors and faculty members can provide to students. For instance, Lunneborg (1985) succinctly suggested that "to say you can do 'anything' with a BA in psychology is as irresponsible as saying there is 'nothing' you can do with it" (p. 22). On the basis of her survey of psychology alumni, she concluded that larger organizations are where the better jobs are, that psychology graduates may not be very happy with those jobs at times, and that additional degrees or training in business administration or computer applications can be most helpful. This advice also makes sense in light of the results of a study of psychology baccalaureates as compared with other majors (Littlepage, Perry, & Hodge, 1990). This study reported that psychology baccalaureates were not doing badly and that psychology majors compare favorably with liberal arts majors but do not do as well as business or science majors (Littlepage et al., 1990). When psychology majors are asked whether they would major in psychology again, most tend to say yes. Around 70% agreed with that response in Lunneborg and Wilson (1985), although that number does vary from study to study (e.g., 44% in Littlepage et al., 1990).

As with most careers with a baccalaureate, the picture for psychology majors is not perfectly glowing, nor is it miserably weak. And even the best data available will still be results of studies based on large groups of people. Your results may vary. In fact, your results will vary. By learning from those who have come before you (i.e., individuals interviewed in this book), you can learn from successful psychology graduates in their own words. You can take advice straight from those who have traveled on the same path you are traveling. Ultimately, your success, satisfaction, and happiness are in your hands, but why not listen to the advice of others? Much of the remainder of this book is just about that—providing advice by providing profiles of psychology baccalaureates, followed by tips for you to make the most of your experience.

Finding the Career That Is Right for You 2

n this chapter, I present some basic information that can help get you started on your journey toward understanding possible career paths.

Tools to Classify Job Titles and Personal Preferences

Since its inception in 1939, the *Dictionary of Occupational Titles* (*DOT*) served as a definitive guide in the United States for collecting and organizing occupational information (Farr & Shatkin, 2007). The *DOT* was quite comprehensive, listing 12,741 occupational titles, and was revised multiple times over the years, with the final revision in 1991. The 1991 *DOT* was then changed and re-formed into O*NET (the Occupational Information Network). O*NET is only available online; you can access it at http://online.onetcenter.org. For an outstanding print reference (with supplemental information about careers and career choices), I recommend the book *O*NET Dictionary of Occupational Titles* (Farr & Shatkin, 2007).

Rather than deal with more than 12,000 occupational titles, O*NET was reorganized by the U.S. Department of Labor into broadly defined job titles; the O*NET database currently contains about 950 job titles (Farr & Shatkin, 2007). The information in an O*NET listing is highly organized; see Figure 2.1 for a sample listing straight from O*NET.

O*NET is an amazing tool because of the variety of searches you can do and the wealth of information available. For example, the InDemand flag alerts you to those occupations that are expecting growth in the next few years. Also, the median wages can be helpful, especially for comparisons across occupational categories (remember that the median is the score that divides the distribution in half, so the median income is that which half the workers make more than and half the workers make less than). A person's actual wage will of course vary because of previous experience, the part of the country in which they are working, and so forth. But the median salary data are quite useful for making comparisons.

One of the true strengths of O*NET is the ability to search via multiple fields. For example, if you know the code for the occupation of interest, you can search by the code (e.g., 21-1011.00 is the code for substance abuse and behavioral disorder counselors). You can also search on high-growth industries. As of this writing, the high-growth industries most related to psychology baccalaureates are biotechnology, health care, homeland security, and information technology (with health care being the category most closely associated with the interests of psychology majors). You can also search by job zone (level of education, experience, and training necessary) and job family (although health care is a popular option for psychology baccalaureates, it is certainly not the only option). The search tools for O*NET are impressive, and I encourage you to explore this resource to customize your search for job information and opportunities that best fit your interests.

Holland's Self-Directed Search Codes: Realistic, Investigative, Artistic, Social, Enterprising, and Conventional

The organizational scheme that I have used for this book centers on Holland's (1994) Self-Directed Search (SDS) and the classification codes it uses to organize six different groupings of career types. The basic notion of this theory is that people are happier and more successful in

FIGURE 2.1

Summary Report for:
21-1011.00 - Substance Abuse and Behavioral Disorder Counselors

Counsel and advise individuals with alcohol, tobacco, drug, or other problems, such as gambling and eating disorders. May counsel individuals, families, or groups or engage in prevention programs.

Sample of reported job titles: Counselor, Substance Abuse Counselor (SA Counselor), Chemical Dependency Counselor (CD Counselor), Clinical Counselor, Addictions Counselor, Case Manager, Assessment Specialist, Alcohol and Drug Counselor, Chemical Dependency Professional, Clinician

View report: Summary Details Custom

Tasks I Tools & Technology I Knowledge I Skills I Abilities I Work Activities I Work Context I Job Zone I Interests I Work Styles I Work Values I Related Occupations I Wages & Employment

Tasks

- Counsel clients and patients, individually and in group sessions, to assist in overcoming dependencies, adjusting to life, and making changes.
- Complete and maintain accurate records and reports regarding the patients' histories and progress, services provided, and other required information.
- Develop client treatment plans based on research, clinical experience, and client histories.
- Review and evaluate clients' progress in relation to measurable goals described in treatment and care plans.
- Interview clients, review records, and confer with other professionals to evaluate individuals' mental and physical condition, and to determine their suitability for participation in a specific program.
- Intervene as advocate for clients or patients to resolve emergency problems in crisis situations.
- Provide clients or family members with information about addiction issues and about available services and programs, making appropriate referrals when necessary.
- Modify treatment plans to comply with changes in client status.
- Coordinate counseling efforts with mental health professionals and other health professionals such as doctors, nurses, and social workers.
- Attend training sessions to increase knowledge and skills.

Tools & Technology
Tools used in this occupation:

Sample O*NET listing. O*NET = Occupational Information Network. O*NET™ is a trademark of the U.S. Department of Labor, Employment and Training Administration. From the O*NET database available at http://www.onetcenter.org/tools.html. In the public domain.

FIGURE 2.1 *(Continued)*

Alcohol analysers — Breathalyzers

Desktop computers

Notebook computers

Personal computers

Personal digital assistant PDAs or organizers — Personal digital assistants PDA

Technology used in this occupation:

Data base user interface and query software — Database software; EAG Economic Analysis Group CaseTrack; Online informational database software

Medical software — Addison Health Systems WritePad EMR Systems; Client System; STI Computer Services ChartMaker; Varian Medical Systems software

Presentation software

Spreadsheet software — Microsoft Excel

Word processing software — Microsoft Word

Knowledge

Therapy and Counseling — Knowledge of principles, methods, and procedures for diagnosis, treatment, and rehabilitation of physical and mental dysfunctions, and for career counseling and guidance.

Psychology — Knowledge of human behavior and performance; individual differences in ability, personality, and interests; learning and motivation; psychological research methods; and the assessment and treatment of behavioral and affective disorders.

Sociology and Anthropology — Knowledge of group behavior and dynamics, societal trends and influences, human migrations, ethnicity, cultures and their history and origins.

Customer and Personal Service — Knowledge of principles and processes for providing customer and personal services. This includes customer needs assessment, meeting quality standards for services, and evaluation of customer satisfaction.

Education and Training — Knowledge of principles and methods for curriculum and training design, teaching and instruction for individuals and groups, and the measurement of training effects.

English Language — Knowledge of the structure and content of the English language including the meaning and spelling of words, rules of composition, and grammar.

Sample O*NET listing. O*NET = Occupational Information Network. O*NET™ is a trademark of the U.S. Department of Labor, Employment and Training Administration. From the O*NET database available at http://www.onetcenter.org/tools.html. In the public domain.

FIGURE 2.1 *(Continued)*

Philosophy and Theology — Knowledge of different philosophical systems and religions. This includes their basic principles, values, ethics, ways of thinking, customs, practices, and their impact on human culture.

Administration and Management — Knowledge of business and management principles involved in strategic planning, resource allocation, human resources modeling, leadership technique, production methods, and coordination of people and resources.

Law and Government — Knowledge of laws, legal codes, court procedures, precedents, government regulations, executive orders, agency rules, and the democratic political process.

Clerical — Knowledge of administrative and clerical procedures and systems such as word processing, managing files and records, stenography and transcription, designing forms, and other office procedures and terminology.

Skills

Active Listening — Giving full attention to what other people are saying, taking time to understand the points being made, asking questions as appropriate, and not interrupting at inappropriate times.

Social Perceptiveness — Being aware of others' reactions and understanding why they react as they do.

Service Orientation — Actively looking for ways to help people.

Speaking — Talking to others to convey information effectively.

Time Management — Managing one's own time and the time of others.

Critical Thinking — Using logic and reasoning to identify the strengths and weaknesses of alternative solutions, conclusions or approaches to problems.

Persuasion — Persuading others to change their minds or behavior.

Reading Comprehension — Understanding written sentences and paragraphs in work related documents.

Instructing — Teaching others how to do something.

Writing — Communicating effectively in writing as appropriate for the needs of the audience.

Abilities

Oral Comprehension — The ability to listen to and understand information and ideas presented through spoken words and sentences.

Sample O*NET listing. O*NET = Occupational Information Network. O*NET™ is a trademark of the U.S. Department of Labor, Employment and Training Administration. From the O*NET database available at http://www.onetcenter.org/tools.html. In the public domain.

FIGURE 2.1 (Continued)

Oral Expression — The ability to communicate information and ideas in speaking so others will understand.

Problem Sensitivity — The ability to tell when something is wrong or is likely to go wrong. It does not involve solving the problem, only recognizing there is a problem.

Speech Clarity — The ability to speak clearly so others can understand you.

Inductive Reasoning — The ability to combine pieces of information to form general rules or conclusions (includes finding a relationship among seemingly unrelated events).

Deductive Reasoning — The ability to apply general rules to specific problems to produce answers that make sense.

Speech Recognition — The ability to identify and understand the speech of another person.

Written Comprehension — The ability to read and understand information and ideas presented in writing.

Near Vision — The ability to see details at close range (within a few feet of the observer).

Written Expression — The ability to communicate information and ideas in writing so others will understand.

Work Activities

Getting Information — Observing, receiving, and otherwise obtaining information from all relevant sources.

Assisting and Caring for Others — Providing personal assistance, medical attention, emotional support, or other personal care to others such as coworkers, customers, or patients.

Establishing and Maintaining Interpersonal Relationships — Developing constructive and cooperative working relationships with others, and maintaining them over time.

Communicating with Supervisors, Peers, or Subordinates — Providing information to supervisors, co-workers, and subordinates by telephone, in written form, e-mail, or in person.

Documenting/Recording Information — Entering, transcribing, recording, storing, or maintaining information in written or electronic/magnetic form.

Making Decisions and Solving Problems — Analyzing information and evaluating results to choose the best solution and solve problems.

Organizing, Planning, and Prioritizing Work — Developing specific goals and plans to prioritize, organize, and accomplish your work.

Sample O*NET listing. O*NET = Occupational Information Network. O*NET™ is a trademark of the U.S. Department of Labor, Employment and Training Administration. From the O*NET database available at http://www.onetcenter.org/tools.html. In the public domain.

FIGURE 2.1 (Continued)

Resolving Conflicts and Negotiating with Others — Handling complaints, settling disputes, and resolving grievances and conflicts, or otherwise negotiating with others.

Evaluating Information to Determine Compliance with Standards — Using relevant information and individual judgment to determine whether events or processes comply with laws, regulations, or standards.

Communicating with Persons Outside Organization — Communicating with people outside the organization, representing the organization to customers, the public, government, and other external sources. This information can be exchanged in person, in writing, or by telephone or e-mail.

Work Context

Contact With Others — How much does this job require the worker to be in contact with others (face-to-face, by telephone, or otherwise) in order to perform it?

Face-to-Face Discussions — How often do you have to have face-to-face discussions with individuals or teams in this job?

Telephone — How often do you have telephone conversations in this job?

Indoors, Environmentally Controlled — How often does this job require working indoors in environmentally controlled conditions?

Work With Work Group or Team — How important is it to work with others in a group or team in this job?

Freedom to Make Decisions — How much decision making freedom, without supervision, does the job offer?

Structured versus Unstructured Work — To what extent is this job structured for the worker, rather than allowing the worker to determine tasks, priorities, and goals?

Deal With External Customers — How important is it to work with external customers or the public in this job?

Letters and Memos — How often does the job require written letters and memos?

Spend Time Sitting — How much does this job require sitting?

Job Zone

Title Job Zone Five: Extensive Preparation Needed

Overall Experience Extensive skill, knowledge, and experience are needed for these occupations. Many require more than five years of experience. For example, surgeons must complete four years of college and an additional five to seven years of specialized medical training to be able to do their job.

Sample O*NET listing. O*NET = Occupational Information Network. O*NET™ is a trademark of the U.S. Department of Labor, Employment and Training Administration. From the O*NET database available at http://www.onetcenter.org/tools.html. In the public domain.

FIGURE 2.1 *(Continued)*

Job Training Employees may need some on-the-job training, but most of these occupations assume that the person will already have the required skills, knowledge, work-related experience, and/or training.

Job Zone Examples These occupations often involve coordinating, training, supervising, or managing the activities of others to accomplish goals. Very advanced communication and organizational skills are required. Examples include librarians, lawyers, aerospace engineers, physicists, school psychologists, and surgeons.

SVP Range (8.0 and above)

Education A bachelor's degree is the minimum formal education required for these occupations. However, many also require graduate school. For example, they may require a master's degree, and some require a Ph.D., M.D., or J.D. (law degree).

Interests
Interest code: **SI**

Social — Social occupations frequently involve working with, communicating with, and teaching people. These occupations often involve helping or providing service to others.

Investigative — Investigative occupations frequently involve working with ideas, and require an extensive amount of thinking. These occupations can involve searching for facts and figuring out problems mentally.

Artistic — Artistic occupations frequently involve working with forms, designs and patterns. They often require self-expression and the work can be done without following a clear set of rules.

Work Styles

Integrity — Job requires being honest and ethical.

Concern for Others — Job requires being sensitive to others' needs and feelings and being understanding and helpful on the job.

Dependability — Job requires being reliable, responsible, and dependable, and fulfilling obligations.

Stress Tolerance — Job requires accepting criticism and dealing calmly and effectively with high stress situations.

Self Control — Job requires maintaining composure, keeping emotions in check, controlling anger, and avoiding aggressive behavior, even in very difficult situations.

Cooperation — Job requires being pleasant with others on the job and displaying a good-natured, cooperative attitude.

Sample O*NET listing. O*NET = Occupational Information Network. O*NET™ is a trademark of the U.S. Department of Labor, Employment and Training Administration. From the O*NET database available at http://www.onetcenter.org/tools.html. In the public domain.

FIGURE 2.1 *(Continued)*

Adaptability/Flexibility — Job requires being open to change (positive or negative) and to considerable variety in the workplace.

Initiative — Job requires a willingness to take on responsibilities and challenges.

Persistence — Job requires persistence in the face of obstacles.

Social Orientation — Job requires preferring to work with others rather than alone, and being personally connected with others on the job.

Work Values

Achievement — Occupations that satisfy this work value are results oriented and allow employees to use their strongest abilities, giving them a feeling of accomplishment. Corresponding needs are Ability Utilization and Achievement.

Independence — Occupations that satisfy this work value allow employs to work on their own and make decisions. Corresponding needs are Creativity, Responsibility and Autonomy.

Related Occupations

21-1021.00	Child, Family, and School Social Workers
21-1093.00	Social and Human Service Assistants
29-1122.00	Occupational Therapists InDemand
29-1123.00	Physical Therapists InDemand
29-1125.00	Recreational Therapists
39-9041.00	Residential Advisors

Wages & Employment Trends
National

Median wages (2006)	$16.36 hourly, $34,040 annual
Employment (2004)	76,000 employees
Projected growth (2004-2014)	▪▪▪▪Much faster than average (27+%)
Projected need (2004-2014)	39,000 additional employees

Sample O*NET listing. O*NET = Occupational Information Network. O*NET™ is a trademark of the U.S. Department of Labor, Employment and Training Administration. From the O*NET database available at http://www.onetcenter.org/tools.html. In the public domain.

a job that matches their interests, values, and skills. Scoring of the SDS is linked to occupational codes and titles. Thus, by determining your preferences for styles or types, the SDS gives you some indication of the jobs that you might like and that would make the most of your skills and interests. The fundamental idea is that people and work environments can be classified according to Holland's six types; thus, if you know your own type and understand the types that are associated with particular careers, you can find a match (Landrum & Davis, 2007). See Table 2.1 for the six types, with information about and sample occupations for each (Psychological Assessment Resources, 2001).

Holland's (1994) SDS is relatively straightforward. There is an Internet version (http://www.self-directed-search.com/index.html) that you can take for a small fee and receive a personalized report with your results (I actually did this, and I present a portion of my own report in chapter 11). Individuals answer questions about their aspirations, activities, competencies, occupations, and other self-estimates. These scores yield a three-letter Summary Code that designates the three personality types an individual most closely resembles. With this code, test takers use the Occupations Finder to discover those occupations that best match their personality types, interests, and skills (Landrum & Davis, 2007).

When I sampled for organizations out of the Directory of Associations (2007), I included survey participants from all six of these groups in chapters 3 through 6 (for more about how I collected these data, see chapter 11). Survey respondents classified their career in one of these career categories and also classified their personal preference for a career category, sometimes resulting in a match between the two, but at other times a mismatch. You will see in the coming chapters that there is an unequal distribution of respondents across the six Holland codes; respondents in the online interviews predominately self-identified in the social category, which indeed is the category most closely aligned with psychology and psychologists. Interestingly, the other five categories were also represented, but to a lesser extent than the social category.

Customizing Your Own Career Information

O*NET and other resources like the *O*NET Dictionary of Occupational Titles* (Farr & Shatkin, 2007) can be of great use for finding general information about careers. At some level, however, you will need to focus your search for career information on areas that are more specific

TABLE 2.1

Types and Occupations of the Self-Directed Search

Personality type	Occupations	Personality type	Occupations
Realistic		**Investigative**	
▪ Have mechanical ability and athletic ability. ▪ Like to work outdoors. ▪ Like to work with machines and tools. ▪ Genuine, humble, modest, natural, practical, and realistic.	▪ Aircraft controller ▪ Electrician ▪ Carpenter ▪ Auto mechanic ▪ Surveyor ▪ Rancher	▪ Have math and science abilities. ▪ Like to explore and understand things and events. ▪ Like to work alone and solve problems. ▪ Analytical, curious, intellectual, and rational.	▪ Biologist ▪ Geologist ▪ Anthropologist ▪ Chemist ▪ Medical technologist ▪ Physicist
Artistic		**Social**	
▪ Have artistic skills and a good imagination. ▪ Like reading, music, or art. ▪ Enjoy creating original work. ▪ Expressive, original, idealistic, independent, and open.	▪ Musician ▪ Writer ▪ Decorator ▪ Composer ▪ Stage director ▪ Sculptor	▪ Like to be around other people. ▪ Like to cooperate with other people. ▪ Like to help other people. ▪ Friendly, understanding, cooperative, sociable, and warm.	▪ Teacher ▪ Counselor ▪ Speech therapist ▪ Clergy member ▪ Social worker ▪ Clinical psychologist
Enterprising		**Conventional**	
▪ Have leadership and public speaking ability. ▪ Like to influence other people. ▪ Like to assume responsibility. ▪ Ambitious, extraverted, adventurous, and self-confident.	▪ Manager ▪ Salesperson ▪ Business executive ▪ Buyer ▪ Promoter ▪ Lawyer	▪ Have clerical and math abilities. ▪ Like to work indoors. ▪ Like organizing things and meeting clear standards. ▪ Efficient, practical, orderly, and conscientious.	▪ Banker ▪ Financial analyst ▪ Tax expert ▪ Stenographer ▪ Production editor ▪ Cost estimator

Note. Data from Psychological Assessment Resources (2001).

to you. One strategy that will help with this approach is to complete Holland's (1994) SDS. The O*NET database contains references from occupations that are linked to these codes; sometimes you'll see them referred to as RIASEC codes, standing for the six different occupational categories identified by Holland: (a) realistic, (b) investigative, (c) artistic, (d) social, (e) enterprising, and (f) conventional. (Together, these are known as RIASEC.)

Rajecki (2007) provided a useful guide to creating your own customized career information list (you can find the complete instructions at http://www.teachpsych.org/otrp/resources/rajecki07.pdf). Rajecki made the argument that "in the challenging and sometimes confusing world of career planning, psychology majors and their mentors are more likely to identify potential occupational pathways if they have their own ready access to useful information about a wide variety of jobs" (p. 2), and I couldn't agree more. This resource also provides samples from O*NET and tips for interpreting the information found there, such as understanding the Job Zones and specific vocational preparation ranges. Some of the example job titles recommended for psychology baccalaureates beginning a job search include human resource managers, market research analysts, public relations managers, sales managers, community service managers, and survey researchers (Rajecki, 2007).

Another suggestion (Rajecki, 2007) is to take advantage of the Occupational Outlook Handbook, which is available online at http://www.bls.gov/oco/home.htm. The Occupational Outlook Handbook provides information on hundreds of jobs in the areas of training and education needed, earnings, expected job growth, what workers do, and working conditions. What I like is that the Occupational Outlook Handbook also gives you additional information about job search tips.

Mismatches Between Job Preferences and Holland Codes

The Holland codes (RIASEC) are popularly used throughout the various job and occupational databases available to you. Although online interviewees did not complete the actual SDS, I did ask each one to answer two related questions: (a) In thinking about your current career, which of the following categories would you place your career in? and (b) In thinking about yourself and the way you prefer to interact with the world, which of the following categories would you place yourself in? After seeing the results of the interviews, I became interested in the matches and mismatches between these two items and how they might influence job and career satisfaction. For instance, if you identified your career as conventional but indicated your preference for the way you interact with the world as artistic, would this mismatch lead to lower job satisfaction? Conversely, if your career and your preference matched, would you report higher job satisfaction?

As you read the interviews in the following chapters, pay attention to the individuals who match or mismatch on these last two interview questions. One of the trends that I noticed is that some individuals with mismatches were more likely to wonder about another career or, when asked whether they would do the same thing again, suggested that they might have taken a different route. You should remember that you are not locked in to any job or career for the rest of your life; if you discover after a while that you are unhappy, there are opportunities for retraining or to return to college for more education in a different career area.

How Useful Are the Holland SDS Codes and O*NET Classifications?

I completed the SDS and present my interpretative report in chapter 11. I completed the SDS truthfully, not trying to answer in a particular way or for any illustrative purpose. My RIASEC code is SIR, which means my strongest preference is for social, followed by investigative, followed by realistic. One of the features I like about the *O*NET Dictionary of Occupational Titles* (Farr & Shatkin, 2007) is that it provides an appendix that organizes O*NET occupations by RIASEC two-letter codes. After I completed the SDS and determined my occupational code was SIR, I then looked in the appendix for the matching code (the appendix lists only the first two letters, so I looked under SI). The match between my SDS and the O*NET occupations that SIs tend to prefer is shown in Table 2.2. The outcome demonstrates how a valid and reliable instrument can be immensely useful and how systematic data collection can result in predictive relationships that make sense.

To match occupations to RIASEC codes, researchers interview thousands of individuals and relate how folks in certain occupations also have certain personality preferences. Do you see how it turned out for me? My SDS code is SIR (social–investigative–realistic). Using the appendix in Farr and Shatkin (2007), I looked up potential job titles for SIs. And there I was—25.1066.00, psychology teachers, postsecondary. I match up perfectly! This example demonstrates the practical, applied value of research. By completing the SDS honestly and receiving my score, I can use that score to seek out occupational information. The occupational

TABLE 2.2

Sample Listing of Job Titles That Match Holland (1994) Self-Directed Search Code SI

Job title	O*NET number
Counseling psychologists	19-3031.03
Substance abuse and behavioral disorder counselors	21-1011.00
Mental health counselors	21-1014.00
Medical and public health social workers	21-1022.00
Mental health and substance abuse social workers	21.1023.00
Anthropology and archeology teachers, postsecondary	25-1061.00
Area, ethnic, and cultural studies teachers, postsecondary	25-1062.00
Economics teachers, postsecondary	25-1063.00
Political science teachers, postsecondary	25-1065.00
Psychology teachers, postsecondary	25.1066.00
Sociology teachers, postsecondary	25-1067.00
Nursing instructors and teachers, postsecondary	25-1072.00
History teachers, postsecondary	25-1125.00
Graduate teaching assistants	25-1191.00
Instructional coordinators	25-9031.00
Podiatrists	29-1081.00
Registered nurses	29-1111.00
Audiologists	29-1121.00
Speech–language pathologists	29-1127.00
Orthotists and prosthetists	29-2091.00

Note. O*NET = Occupational Information Network; SI = social–investigative.

information I was able to look up using the O*NET data (Farr & Shatkin, 2007) indicates that the profession I actually chose is listed as one of the many occupations that SI fits well within. I encourage you to also obtain your RIASEC code and explore the career options. This doesn't mean that you are locked into what might be recommended to you, but your RIASEC code can provide helpful information that can guide your search. To be clear, though, your RIASEC code is not an excuse to explore or not explore a career. Those choices are up to you.

IN THEIR OWN WORDS: PROFILES OF PSYCHOLOGY BACCALAUREATES AND THEIR CAREER CHOICES

Early-Career Professionals in Social Fields

3

A fter collecting the data from the online interview process, I quickly realized that when asked to think about their current career and place it in one of six categories, most respondents placed themselves in the social category. The choices that were presented to the interviewees are presented in Table 3.1. Because of the volume of responses in the social category, I decided to divide these responses and present the data across two chapters of this book. This chapter looks at early-career respondents, ages 20 to 34, and the next chapter looks at later-career respondents, ages 35 to 50. Because so many psychology majors end up in careers identified as social, I believe it is important to provide multiple examples of success stories that occur in this category.

Description and Sample Occupations

But what does this social category mean? In Holland's (1994) Self-Directed Search,

> Social (S) people like social careers such as teacher, speech therapist, religious worker, counselor, clinical

TABLE 3.1

Career Categories Used in Survey

Category	Job examples
Social	Teacher, counselor, speech therapist, clergy member, social worker, clinical psychologist
Realistic	Aircraft controller, electrician, carpenter, auto mechanic, surveyor, rancher
Investigative	Biologist, geologist, anthropologist, chemist, medical technologist, physicist
Conventional	Banker, financial analyst, tax expert, stenographer, production editor, cost estimator
Artistic	Musician, writer, decorator, composer, stage director, sculptor
Enterprising	Manager, salesperson, business executive, buyer, promoter, lawyer

psychologist, and nurse. The S type usually likes to be around other people, is interested in how people get along, and likes to help other people with their problems. The S type generally likes to help, teach, and counsel people more than engage in mechanical or technical activity. The S type is described as convincing, cooperative, friendly, generous, helpful, idealistic, kind, patient, responsible, social, sympathetic, tactful, understanding, and warm. (Reardon, n.d., ¶7)

Interviews

By far and away the most interesting and important information for me to present here are the actual interviews with psychology baccalaureates who identified their own careers as being in the social occupational category. There is something quite powerful about reading these interviews. Remember, they have only been lightly edited, and the meaning or intention of any of the statements provided has not been changed. As an organizational mechanism, I present the interviews in interviewee age order, from the youngest interviewee to the oldest in this and the other chapters.

BUSINESS BACKGROUND CAN PROVIDE AN EARLY ADVANTAGE

Your name: Rachel W.
Your age: 20
Your gender: Female

Your primary job title: University relations recruiter
Your current employer: Whirlpool
How long have you been employed in your present position? 3 months
What year did you graduate with your bachelor's degree in psychology? 2007
Describe your major job duties and responsibilities.

- recruiting and attracting new talent from the university setting
- interviewing
- managing hiring processes
- planning and implementing new strategies for gaining candidate interest and building the Whirlpool Brand presence on campuses

What elements of your undergraduate training in psychology do you use in your work?

- personality analysis
- counseling skills
- statistics

What do you like most about your job? Meeting and working with new people.

What do you like least about your job? Sometimes the travel becomes tiring.

What is the compensation package for an entry-level position in your occupation? $38,000 to $60,000

What benefits (e.g., health insurance, pension) are typically available for someone in your profession? Typical for most business settings.

What are the key skills necessary for you to succeed in your career? People skills and strategic thinking.

Thinking back to your undergraduate career, what courses would you recommend that you believe are key to success in your type of career? Social psychology, personality, research methods, counseling.

Thinking back to your undergraduate career, can you think of outside of class activities (e.g., research assistantships, internships, Psi Chi) that were key to success in your type of career? Internships and leadership positions within organizations.

What advice would you give to someone who was thinking about entering the field you are in? Get some business background in addition to psychology. Get internship experience and get involved in organizations including the leadership roles.

If you were choosing a career and occupation all over again, what (if anything) would you do differently? Nothing at this point in my career.

In thinking about your current career, which of the following categories would you place your career in? Social

In thinking about you and the way you prefer to interact with the world, which of the following categories would you place yourself in? Social

Rachel is so early in her new career that she does not offer much advice; this makes sense for someone in their first job after graduation. However, consistent with messages presented in the research literature, Rachel does suggest a business background in addition to psychology. She also mentions internships and leadership positions twice—something to think about as you plan your own undergraduate career majoring in psychology.

HELPING PEOPLE ONE AT A TIME

Your name: Erin B.

Your age: 23

Your gender: Female

Your primary job title: Program coordinator, adolescent pregnancy prevention

Your current employer: Lutheran Services in Iowa

How long have you been employed in your present position? 1 month

What year did you graduate with your bachelor's degree in psychology? 2006

Describe your major job duties and responsibilities. Coordinating activities under a statewide program grant to reduce the number of adolescent pregnancies by going into the community schools and programs and giving lessons and events on the behavioral aspect of pregnancy prevention.

What elements of your undergraduate training in psychology do you use in your work? Understanding, analyzing, and applying statistics; child and adolescent psychology; basic counseling; educational psychology; human sexuality.

What do you like most about your job? I'm a caseworker providing remedial services as well, and I like being able to interact one-on-one with clients.

What do you like least about your job? I feel like I am behind in understanding public policy and law as far as providing mental health care.

Beyond your bachelor's degree, what additional education and/or specialized training have you received? Basically, just on-the-job training.

What is the compensation package for an entry-level position in your occupation? I'm salaried at a little over $24,000 a year, but I have to work a second job to compensate.

What benefits (e.g., health insurance, pension) are typically available for someone in your profession? Health, dental, vision, life, 401(k).

Question to Think About: Are you willing to work a second job to compensate for a low salary?

What are the key skills necessary for you to succeed in your career? A good understanding of the [Department of Health Services] system, lots of networking skills, the ability to get on the same level as your client or the classroom.

Thinking back to your undergraduate career, what courses would you recommend that you believe are key to success in your type of career? Abnormal psychology, educational psychology, statistics, biology, and so forth.

Thinking back to your undergraduate career, can you think of outside of class activities (e.g., research assistantships, internships, Psi Chi, etc.) that were key to success in your type of career? I went to a small private university, so there wasn't a research program in psychology, nor availability for internships.

As an undergraduate, do you wish you had done anything differently? If so, what? Honestly, I probably might have chosen a different career path, like public health.

What advice would you give to someone who was thinking about entering the field you are in? You have to really want to go into the human services field or be willing to go to graduate school right away. An undergraduate degree in psychology transitions well into other academic fields.

If you were choosing a career and occupation all over again, what (if anything) would you do differently? I'd maybe have taken a skills and personality assessment earlier on as an undergraduate, so I would be more aware of where my strengths are and go into a more clinical field.

In thinking about your current career, which of the following categories would you place your career in? Social

In thinking about you and the way you prefer to interact with the world, which of the following categories would you place yourself in? Realistic

Erin is candid in first emphasizing the importance of understanding, analyzing, and applying statistics (see, you really can use these skills in the real world). Second, Erin is honest about her career path—thinking back on it, she might have chosen public health. Given that she is so early into her career, this ambivalence is normal; also, throughout the interviews you'll see that folks who mismatch tend to think about opportunities other than their current position. The more you know what you want to do, the better you can design your undergraduate experiences to match those goals. Another early theme identified here are those students who mention abnormal psychology; throughout the next four chapters, many interviewees mention this course.

SUCCESS IS IN THE DETAILS

Your name: Danielle M.
Your age: 25
The name of your professional association? STAR Academy-QUEST
Your primary job title: Lead youth counselor
Your current employer: State of South Dakota
How long have you been employed in your present position? 2½ years
What year did you graduate with your bachelor's degree in psychology? 2005

Describe your major job duties and responsibilities. The following are some of my job duties and responsibilities:

- [Have] taken on the role as senior counselor (make sure everyone is abiding by our policies).
- Scheduling.
- Process Major Incident Reports.
- Maintain physical custody of each assigned youth through direct supervision and accountability of activities to ensure each youth is protected from physical, emotional, sexual, or psychological abuse or mistreatment.
- Plan and supervise recreational, social, spiritual, and daily living activities for youth.
- Intervene in disputes between youths, stop physical and verbal confrontations, and intervene and deescalate crisis situations.
- PBS coordinator (statistics for our performance and student demographics).
- Organize and implement large and small groups.
- Assess youth on entering the program.
- Establish individual treatment plans.
- Evaluate individuals' progress in the program.
- Establish and maintain contact with those involved in the youth's life.
- Motivational interviewing trainer.
- Work with various resources in the community to assist in reintegrating the youth.
- Established new formats for required documents.

What elements of your undergraduate training in psychology do you use in your work?

- All psychology components have assisted me in understanding my clients' mental health issues and status, so I can best meet their needs.
- Research and statistics.

What do you like most about your job? Being able to give my clients the tools that will enable them to lead successful, healthy lifestyles. Also, giving them the hope and inspiration to break out of the negative lifestyle cycle.

What do you like least about your job? Not having the resources to give them all the help they need.

Beyond your bachelor's degree, what additional education and/or specialized training have you received? I have training in the following:

- Corrective thinking
- Gangs

- Motivational interviewing
- Science-based drug education
- Honoring Children, Respectful Ways: Treatment of American Indian and Alaska Native Children With Sexual Behavior Problems
- What Works in Reducing Recidivism for Youth and Adults, presented by Dr. Edward Latessa
- Offering Hope to Victims in the Spirit of Justice
- Crisis prevention and intervention
- Manager and leadership training
- Conflict management for women
- Youth risk conferences (eating disorders, self-harming, teen dating violence, drugs/alcohol, values, youth work ethic)
- Adolescent development

What is the compensation package for an entry-level position in your occupation? The starting hourly wage for a youth counselor is $14.89. The starting hourly wage for a wellness instructor is $15.12.

What benefits (e.g., health insurance, pension) are typically available for someone in your profession? Health insurance, dental/vision, travel reimbursement, paid training, paid sick and vacation, paid holidays, 401(k)

What are the key skills necessary for you to succeed in your career?

- Educational background
- In-depth understanding of juveniles and the diversity of juvenile offenders and their families
- Communication skills, which includes patience, reasoning, conflict resolution, and reflective listening
- People skills: ability to work with various people in various situations, meaning being able to step out of your comfort zone
- Computer skills

Thinking back to your undergraduate career, what courses would you recommend that you believe are key to success in your type of career?

- General psychology
- Adolescent psychology
- Developmental psychology
- Social psychology
- Abnormal psychology
- Juvenile delinquency
- Juvenile law
- Corrections and treatment for juvenile offenders
- Forensic social work: treatment programs
- Culture and psychology

Question to Think About: Think about these starting wages. Is this amount something you could live on?

- Drugs, alcohol, and crime
- Behavioral statistics
- Multicultural issues
- Any classes that require a lot of report/research writing

Thinking back to your undergraduate career, can you think of outside of class activities (e.g., research assistantships, internships, Psi Chi) that were key to success in your type of career?

- Psychology Club
- Criminal Justice Club
- Tours of different correctional facilities
- My internship, which was at my current place of employment
- Volunteer work with at-risk youth

What advice would you give to someone who was thinking about entering the field you are in? To get as much hands-on experience as possible so you can relate how the knowledge and concepts relate to working with the youth. Also, to get involved in as many activities/programs as you can because the exposure to different ideas assists in becoming a more rounded person.

If you were choosing a career and occupation all over again, what (if anything) would you do differently? I would get my master's prior to entering the work field.

In thinking about your current career, which of the following categories would you place your career in? Social

In thinking about you and the way you prefer to interact with the world, which of the following categories would you place yourself in? Social

Danielle provides detailed responses, giving us a realistic view of what her job is like and what her responsibilities are. When giving advice, Danielle suggests getting as much hands-on experience as possible so that you can connect knowledge to actual working conditions. Using the internship opportunities that are available to you is a great way to get some hands-on experience, usually in the community, often for credit, and sometimes even paid. If you carefully read her job responsibilities, you can see that this position will really help Danielle grow, and grow quickly. These skills and abilities will be valuable to Danielle and will help her market herself, whether in her current position or eventually in looking elsewhere for employment.

APPLIES PSYCHOLOGY EVERY DAY

Your name: Nicole R.
Your age: 27
Your gender: Female
Your primary job title: Service coordinator—Services for People with Disabilities

Your current employer: Lutheran Services in Iowa

What year did you graduate with your bachelor's degree in psychology? 2002

Describe your major job duties and responsibilities. Oversee and manage all services within Services for People With Disabilities service line. This includes budgeting, training, supervision of supervisory and direct-line staff, maintaining and ensuring quality of service and case files, developing and implementing procedures, acting as liaison and representative of agency in meetings and public appearances, and so forth.

What elements of your undergraduate training in psychology do you use in your work? Psychology is a great tool. I use it in my everyday relations with my staff, funders, consumers, and family. We serve many adults and children with chronic mental illness, and my training in psychology has been of great assistance in training others as well as offering advice and support to both consumers/families and staff. Knowledge of medications has been infinitely useful as well.

What do you like most about your job? Every day is a new day with new challenges. This is not a cookie-cutter job.

What do you like least about your job? Rarely seeing concrete results of the work I do. It's not like working in retail or sales. It is hard to determine sometimes how successful I am without looking at revenues and expenses.

Beyond your bachelor's degree, what additional education and/or specialized training have you received? Pretty much anything available: medication manager, mandatory dependent adult and child abuse reporting, cardiopulmonary resuscitation (CPR), first aid, defensive driving, employment law, brain injury training, Mandt, self-defense, deescalation, ethics, [Health Insurance Portability and Accountability Act], [Occupational Safety and Health Administration], universal precautions.

What benefits (e.g., health insurance, pension) are typically available for someone in your profession? Medical, dental, short- and long-term disability, cafeteria plan, 401(k).

What are the key skills necessary for you to succeed in your career? Compassion, attention to detail, meeting deadlines, and inquisitiveness.

Thinking back to your undergraduate career, what courses would you recommend that you believe are key to success in your type of career?

- Abnormal psychology
- Theory of criminal justice—I know that sounds weird, but the course was more of an investigation of yourself than learning and regurgitating theory. I got to know myself there.
- Online courses—they taught me real-world need to be more self-directed.

Thinking back to your undergraduate career, can you think of outside of class activities (e.g., research assistantships, internships, Psi Chi) that were key to

Question to Think About: Have you ever thought about how you might benefit from the format of a course (such as an online course)?

success in your type of career? Not necessarily in my career. Although they look great on a résumé, I don't feel that they were key components to obtaining my current (or previous) position.

As an undergraduate, do you wish you had done anything differently? If so, what? Gotten more involved with my professors. Only a few knew my name at the time, and I doubt I would be remembered today.

What advice would you give to someone who was thinking about entering the field you are in? It's overwhelming, but rewarding. Don't let the little things get you down. Set your goals and work for them. Oh, and "to-do" lists—they're a great way to measure where you've been and where you need to be.

If you were choosing a career and occupation all over again, what (if anything) would you do differently? I might have become a pharmacist, I guess. However, who's to say that I would wake up every day wanting to go to work? I get that now, so why spend my time with "what ifs?"

In thinking about your current career, which of the following categories would you place your career in? Social

In thinking about you and the way you prefer to interact with the world, which of the following categories would you place yourself in? Social

First off, Nicole reminds us that "every day is a new day with new challenges. This is not a cookie-cutter job." One of the great aspects of a bachelor's degree in psychology is the ability to think critically. With honed critical thinking skills, you can adapt to changing job demands and challenges. When thinking about what she would have done differently, Nicole wishes that she had worked more with professors and gotten to know them better. This is advice you can take now, and make changes before it is too late. Also, Nicole mentions a theme that reoccurs throughout other interviews—spending little time on regret. She does mention thinking about being a pharmacist, but realizes that spending time considering "what ifs" is not time well spent.

When asked about what she likes least about her job, Nicole mentions the lack of instant results. When we choose to help people, we often don't know whether we are successful, or even when that success might occur. Someone in construction has that (relatively) instant gratification of seeing what he or she has built. However, health care professionals, educators, and others often don't receive feedback on their success. Or, in Nicole's case, her clients may be successful years later, but Nicole won't have that knowledge. Also, Nicole learned much as an undergraduate in a class she didn't expect to—theories of criminal justice. Keeping an open mind about the classes you are enrolled in may lead to enlightenment in unexpected venues.

Question to Think About: Think about all these tasks! Could you do this job? Would you like to?

BIG RESPONSIBILITIES, ATTENTION TO DETAIL

Your name: Craig H.
Your age: 29
Your gender: Male
Your primary job title: Level 5 mentor field instructor
Your current employer: Second Nature Blue Ridge (SNBR)
How long have you been employed in your present position? 4 years
What year did you graduate with your bachelor's degree in psychology? 2004
Describe your major job duties and responsibilities.

- Confront students about patterns in their choices, while maintaining unconditional positive regard.
- Teach students positive coping mechanisms utilizing assertive communication, self-awareness, and taking accountability for one's actions.
- Responsible for maintaining student and staff safety.
- Work in conjunction with therapists to facilitate students' treatment plans.
- Instruct psychoeducational groups to encourage positive mental health.
- Teach students about local history and environmental sciences.
- Facilitate staff development through formal feedback groups, evaluations, and competency-based assessment.
- Attend weekly meetings addressing trends in students and staff.
- Design and implement staff trainings.
- Work with students and their families on completion of our program.
- Educate parents about assertive communication and boundary holding.
- Work with families addressing past issues while maintaining a solution-focused approach.
- Assist families in creating cultures that will promote success for the entire family.

What elements of your undergraduate training in psychology do you use in your work? Fundamental understanding of various psychological disorders.

What do you like most about your job? Working with youth.

What do you like least about your job? Scheduling. I work 8 days on with 6 days off year round.

Beyond your bachelor's degree, what additional education and/or specialized training have you received? Bachelor's in outdoor education, emphasis in therapeutic use of adventure; SOLO Wilderness first responder, American Red Cross first aid/CPR responder, Leave No Trace Trainer, Positive

Control Systems crisis intervention training On Rope 1 Basic Vertical Ropes Training Project, WET training, Project WILD training.

What is the compensation package for an entry-level position in your occupation? After the training, you will be participating in a three-rotation internship required of all trainees at $93 per day. After completing the internship, you become a Level 1 field instructor. There are five different levels of field instructors, and your wage will be dependent on your level. These wages vary from Level 1 pay at $98 per day up to $169 per day as the highest level senior/mentor. Advancing in levels is accomplished by fulfilling all of the requirements outlined by the field directors and the therapists. After working 6 consecutive months, you will receive a bonus for completing your commitment, and you will continue receiving bonuses every 3 months thereafter. Bonuses range anywhere from $300 to $700 depending on your level and how many months you have worked with the company.

What benefits (e.g., health insurance, pension) are typically available for someone in your profession? Medical and dental insurance is offered to all field instructors, whether seasonal or full time. You simply fill out an insurance form provided by Second Nature, and you will be added to our company insurance plan 60 days from your first day of employment. SNBR will also require employees to participate in certain training courses for level advancement, such as deescalation training and some medical training like the Wilderness First Responder. These will either be paid for or you will be reimbursed by SNBR on successful completion. SNBR field instructors are offered pro deals with certain outdoor gear companies to purchase necessary gear for field. We also offer a 20% discount on everything in a local gear retailer.

What are the key skills necessary for you to succeed in your career? SNBR looks for individuals with great people skills, ability to work as a team and work under stressful situations if they arise. Field instructors have varied backgrounds and education, and the diversity is welcomed and promoted by SNBR. To work for SNBR, you must be at least 21 years of age. You need to also be certified in basic first aid and CPR or greater (wilderness first responder, emergency medical technician). SNBR seeks people who have wilderness experience. It is preferable that you have fairly extensive backpacking experience. This experience can be either professional or personal. You will be backpacking and hiking your entire shift anywhere from 2 to 8 miles a day with a backpack. SNBR does not use cabins or have a base camp; you will be moving campsites almost every day. Experience with youth, counseling, teaching, previous wilderness experience, or participation in similar activities can benefit an individual to acquire a position at SNBR. Whether it is volunteer or professional experience, it is valuable. SNBR will also offer in-house training from which you will be able to learn communication skills, crisis interventions, and many more tools that you will use working with teens. SNBR also asks that you make a commitment of working in the field for at least 6 to 8 months.

Thinking back to your undergraduate career, what courses would you recommend that you believe are key to success in your type of career? Developmental psychology, behavior modification, and psychopharmacology.

Thinking back to your undergraduate career, can you think of outside of class activities (e.g., research assistantships, internships, Psi Chi) that were key to success in your type of career? Attending the Association of Experiential Education conferences.

What advice would you give to someone who was thinking about entering the field you are in? Conduct a few site visitations before submitting your résumés.

In thinking about your current career, which of the following categories would you place your career in? Social

In thinking about you and the way you prefer to interact with the world, which of the following categories would you place yourself in? Artistic

Craig provides a lot of detail about his job. With this kind of context, you can imagine what his job would look like. Although Craig has an additional degree in outdoor recreation, I wanted to include him because a double major is often a great route by which to expand your career options (obviously, you can expand those options with graduate school, but also without graduate school). Craig also mentions the importance of attending a professional conference; I encourage you to consult with your advisor or mentor to discover how attending (and better yet, presenting at) a conference can open up opportunities for you.

DOUBLE MAJOR MAY EXPAND EMPLOYMENT OPTIONS

Your name: Allison S.

Your age: 30

Your gender: Female

The name of your professional association? Certified psychiatric rehabilitation practitioner

Your primary job title: Intensive psychiatric rehabilitation practitioner

Your current employer: Hope Haven

How long have you been employed in your present position? 6 years

What year did you graduate with your bachelor's degree in psychology? 2001

Describe your major job duties and responsibilities. Work with people with psychiatric disabilities in both group and individual sessions to enhance their life in work, living, social, or educational environments.

What elements of your undergraduate training in psychology do you use in your work? Most all of the classes I took minus the research methods.

What do you like most about your job? Working with the people.

What do you like least about your job? Other providers' thoughts about how we are trying to better the lives of our clients.

What is the compensation package for an entry-level position in your occupation? I currently make $14/hour after 6 years.

What benefits (e.g., health insurance, pension) are typically available for someone in your profession? I get health insurance partially paid for, 403(b) with matching funds up to 8%, disability insurance option, [health savings account].

What are the key skills necessary for you to succeed in your career? Multitasking, genuine caring for people, determination, belief in yourself and others.

Thinking back to your undergraduate career, what courses would you recommend that you believe are key to success in your type of career? Abnormal psychology

Thinking back to your undergraduate career, can you think of outside of class activities (e.g., research assistantships, internships, Psi Chi) that were key to success in your type of career? I worked all through college at the same employer that I am currently employed at now, so the relationships [I] formed were crucial.

As an undergraduate, do you wish you had done anything differently? If so, what? I should have double majored to offer more employment options.

What advice would you give to someone who was thinking about entering the field you are in? Be prepared for an underpaying job with the benefits of working nights and weekends.

If you were choosing a career and occupation all over again, what (if anything) would you do differently? Hard to say; I would like to think that I would do the same thing over again except to maybe go on for a master's degree or go to medical school for psychiatry, but after having a family you don't have time for that.

In thinking about your current career, which of the following categories would you place your career in? Social

In thinking about you and the way you prefer to interact with the world, which of the following categories would you place yourself in? Realistic

Well, Allison uses information from almost all of her classes, except research methods (which makes me smile because it is a class I teach). Allison also had a job lined up before graduating, which had to have made that college-to-career transition (mentioned in chap. 1) very smooth. She also mentions the benefit of double majoring and wishes that she had. Finally, Allison mentions the decisions and sacrifices to be considered in career choices: She thought about continuing her education post-baccalaureate, but felt like having a family would not leave her time for that. This is a serious consideration that you must make individually; depending on your family situation, you may be able to attend graduate school with family in tow, but in other situations it might not be prudent. Allison made the decision not to attend. I also think that Allison's advice to double major makes sense with regard to expanding employment options.

POLITICS ON A COLLEGE CAMPUS

Your name: Hannah M.

Your age: 31

Your gender: Female

The name of your professional association? Association of Fundraising Professionals

Your primary job title: Director of alumni relations and development

Your current employer: Lyndon State College

How long have you been employed in your present position? 2 years

What year did you graduate with your bachelor's degree in psychology? 1997

Describe your major job duties and responsibilities. Alumni relations (e.g., alumni magazine, alumni Web site, alumni socials/gatherings, homecoming, golf tournament, Senior Week events) and development (Annual Fund, Phonathon).

What elements of your undergraduate training in psychology do you use in your work? Communication and networking skills; the patience and skills to work with people from various backgrounds. Leadership training

What do you like most about your job? Meeting alumni from all walks of life. Learning their stories and celebrating their accomplishments.

What do you like least about your job? The pressure of fundraising. The politics on a college campus—too many committees, unions, and so forth.

Beyond your bachelor's degree, what additional education and/or specialized training have you received? Workshops and conferences at all positions I have held. Served as Miss Vermont for 1 year.

What is the compensation package for an entry-level position in your occupation? $41,500 was my starting salary.

What benefits (e.g., health insurance, pension) are typically available for someone in your profession? The benefits with my present employer are tremendous—health, dental, etc. as well as 12% of my salary for retirement (no match required). If you work here 20 years, you have health insurance for life. I am also able to take classes at no cost.

What are the key skills necessary for you to succeed in your career? Communication (oral/written), networking, leadership, organization, confidence, pride in the college.

Thinking back to your undergraduate career, what courses would you recommend that you believe are key to success in your type of career? I think it's very wise to take courses outside your intended major. For example, I took classes in television/communications, education, and exercise science. It gives you a broader base to draw from and opens your eyes to the career paths that others will take.

Thinking back to your undergraduate career, can you think of outside of class activities (e.g., research assistantships, internships, Psi Chi) that were key to success in your type of career? I was involved in many extracurricular activities, [including] being an Alumni Ambassador, which connected me with my

Question to Think About: Have you thought about opportunities to double-major?

predecessor in this position. This type of networking early on has served me well.

As an undergraduate, do you wish you had done anything differently? If so, what? I wish I had doubled majored in psychology and television.

What advice would you give to someone who was thinking about entering the field you are in? I think that a degree in psychology is applicable to many career paths. My degree has prepared me for a variety of jobs: case manager/mental health, social worker/hospital, fundraising events manager, and now director of alumni relations and development.

If you were choosing a career and occupation all over again, what (if anything) would you do differently? As stated above, I wish I had double majored in something broad like psychology and something specific like TV/communications. I'd really like to get into TV, but at this point it would be difficult because of the specific training that is needed.

In thinking about your current career, which of the following categories would you place your career in? Social

In thinking about you and the way you prefer to interact with the world, which of the following categories would you place yourself in? Social

Hannah provides some great answers for us to consider. First, in working for a college, she notes the political atmosphere and the emphasis on fundraising in her position. Second, self-confidence in this type of work is crucial, and her experience as Miss Vermont must have been excellent in preparing her to interact with all different types of people. Having the poise to be in public and make presentations is invaluable to a future successful career. Third, her starting salary is not too far off what new psychology PhDs are offered as starting salaries. Finally, Hannah echoes a theme we have heard before—how she wishes she had double majored. Obviously, Hannah's undergraduate preparation prepared her for a wealth of careers, and she obviously took advantage of the opportunities provided to her.

This is just part of the sampling of online interviews with individuals who self-identified with the social category of occupations. Because there were so many, I presented the younger individuals in this chapter; in the next chapter, I present the older individuals in this category. What are our themes so far? Double majoring is a recurring theme. Abnormal psychology appears vital for those in the helping professions. Finally, you need to truly think about what you want during your undergraduate career. You can certainly retrain and go back to school after graduating if your interests change, but in the grand scheme of things, is it easier to readjust during your undergraduate career than afterward. A bit of thoughtfulness now, such as talking with advisors and taking advantage of internship opportunities, may save you from later regret.

Middle- and Later-Career Professionals in the Social Fields | 4

B ecause of the volume of responses in the social occupational category, I decided to divide these responses and present the data across two chapters of this book. This chapter presents the interviews for those ages 35–50. Because so many psychology majors end up in careers identified as social, I believe it is important to provide multiple examples of success stories in this category.

As a quick reminder, in Holland's (1974) Self-Directed Search,

> Social (S) people like social careers such as teacher, speech therapist, religious worker, counselor, clinical psychologist, and nurse. The S type usually likes to be around other people, is interested in how people get along, and likes to help other people with their problems. The S type generally likes to help, teach, and counsel people more than engage in mechanical or technical activity. The S type is described as convincing, cooperative, friendly, generous, helpful, idealistic, kind, patient, responsible, social, sympathetic, tactful, understanding, and warm. (Reardon, n.d., ¶7)

Interviews

In this section I present the interviews in order of age, from youngest (35) to oldest (55).

QUICK TO THINK, CARE IN RESPONDING

Your name: Pete D.
Your age: 35
Your gender: Male
Your primary job title: Psychiatric rehabilitation specialist
Your current employer: Hope Haven, Inc.
How long have you been employed in your present position? 6 years
What year did you graduate with your bachelor's degree in psychology? 1997
Describe your major job duties and responsibilities. Provide direct service and support to individual adults, children, and/or families with mental illness issues to ensure stability and community integration. Provide crisis management support. Participate in psychiatric consults. Act as resource. Promote recovery and rehabilitation to all individuals served.

What elements of your undergraduate training in psychology do you use in your work? I find myself using a lot of what I learned in my intro to counseling class; however, I also find myself reminded of tidbits throughout my day that remind me of something that I learned in college.

What do you like most about your job? Being one on one with an individual and seeing them blossom into what God has made them to be.

What do you like least about your job? The paperwork.

Beyond your bachelor's degree, what additional education and/or specialized training have you received? I continue to go to seminars. I try to keep them varied so that I am learning about many different things.

What is the compensation package for an entry-level position in your occupation? Similar to higher end factory work. Being a nonprofit agency, the retirement package is above average.

What benefits (e.g., health insurance, pension) are typically available for someone in your profession? Group insurance through the employer, 403(b), vacation days.

What are the key skills necessary for you to succeed in your career? Knowledge of the mental illnesses. Ability to read a situation. Ability to understand an individual's "person." Quick thinking and slow response. Hope.

Thinking back to your undergraduate career, what courses would you recommend that you believe are key to success in your type of career? Intro to counseling.

Thinking back to your undergraduate career, can you think of outside of class activities (e.g., research assistantships, internships, Psi Chi) that were key to success in your type of career? Presenting a theories paper at a conference.

> **Question to Think About:** Are there opportunities in your undergraduate program to present research at a conference?

As an undergraduate, do you wish you had done anything differently? If so, what? I wish I had my part-time job in my field earlier (I began in the field my senior year) than when I did.

What advice would you give to someone who was thinking about entering the field you are in? Get a job within the field to see what it is like. The knowledge went from head knowledge to real-life experience when I worked in the field. My studies became "alive." I would also encourage people to strongly considering working for a year before entering graduate school to help that person break down in which direction they want to focus.

If you were choosing a career and occupation all over again, what (if anything) would you do differently? Begin taking at least on a part-time schedule some graduate school courses soon after graduating.

In thinking about your current career, which of the following categories would you place your career in? Social

In thinking about you and the way you prefer to interact with the world, which of the following categories would you place yourself in? Social

Pete shares his very real experience with us. There is a very caring and sensitive side to those who work with people with mental illness. I found it insightful that one of the key skills Pete felt was necessary for success in his career was hope. Introduction to counseling was an important class for Pete, and he also mentions the benefit of his presenting a paper at a conference while still an undergraduate. Pete also strongly encourages getting a job in the field you think you want to pursue, so that you can see the connection between book knowledge and the real world.

Many of you may pursue a good job with your bachelor's degree at first but later decide to attend graduate school. Working in the real world can be an advantage—you will have experiences that you can share in your graduate studies, and older students often have a greater appreciation for educational opportunities than traditional-age students.

REWARDS IN HELPING OTHERS CHANGE BEHAVIOR

Your name: Shelli R.
Your age: 35
Your gender: Female
Your primary job title: Program coordinator
Your current employer: Christian Opportunity Center
How long have you been employed in your present position? Five months; consulted for 5 months prior
What year did you graduate with your bachelor's degree in psychology? 1994

Describe your major job duties and responsibilities. I coordinate services for individuals with mental retardation who live in our [Intermediate Care Facility for the Mentally Retarded] programs.

What elements of your undergraduate training in psychology do you use in your work? Elementary principles of behavior, statistics, and abnormal psychology are the three courses that stand out that I use daily.

What do you like most about your job? I get to interact with the clients on my caseload daily. I problem solve regularly and coach staff on effective ways to deal with problem behaviors.

What do you like least about your job? The high direct support staff turnover, which results in inconsistency in programming.

Beyond your bachelor's degree, what additional education and/or specialized training have you received? [Crisis Prevention Intervention] training

What is the compensation package for an entry-level position in your occupation? $13–$14 per hour.

What benefits (e.g., health insurance, pension) are typically available for someone in your profession? Health insurance, life insurance, paid time off, profit sharing, flexible benefits plan, educational assistance.

What are the key skills necessary for you to succeed in your career? Patience, listening, problem solving, being able to see the big picture, communicate effectively within a team.

Thinking back to your undergraduate career, what courses would you recommend that you believe are key to success in your type of career? Elementary principles of behavior, or any course that addresses changing behavior.

As an undergraduate, do you wish you had done anything differently? If so, what? Pursued more business courses.

What advice would you give to someone who was thinking about entering the field you are in? Not a field that you would choose for monetary benefits, a field that has far greater rewards.

In thinking about your current career, which of the following categories would you place your career in? Social

In thinking about you and the way you prefer to interact with the world, which of the following categories would you place yourself in? Social

Shelli echoes a theme that we saw in the previous chapter: She wishes she had pursued more business classes. Her advice is also quite telling— "not a field you would choose for monetary benefits, a field that has far greater rewards." Shelli recommends abnormal psychology, a theme we also saw in the previous chapter.

GAINING CULTURAL COMPETENCY

Your name: Phoenix P.
Your age: 35
Your gender: Female
Your primary job title: Legal program coordinator

Question to Think About: Consider for a moment the emotional toll it must take to work with battered women, even though the rewards of helping can be satisfying. Could you handle this emotional toll?

Your current employer: Support Network for Battered Women

How long have you been employed in your present position? 7 months

What year did you graduate with your bachelor's degree in psychology? 2002

Describe your major job duties and responsibilities. Coordinate legal services to English-speaking clients; make referrals for outside legal assistance; supervise and train legal volunteers; train staff on court procedures, accompaniment, and restraining order applications; provide empathic counseling and support; and advocacy as needed with outside agencies.

What elements of your undergraduate training in psychology do you use in your work? Various communication techniques, understanding of a variety of psychological disorders and conditions, and some widely used medications.

What do you like most about your job? Variety and flexibility, knowing I am helping people.

What do you like least about your job? Vicarious traumatization.

Beyond your bachelor's degree, what additional education and/or specialized training have you received? Some master's-level courses in play therapy techniques, coaching, multiple professional level trainings within domestic violence, and certified domestic violence counselor training for state of California (40-plus hours).

What is the compensation package for an entry-level position in your occupation? I get 15 days of vacation, 90% benefits paid, 10 holidays, and 12 sick days per year.

What benefits (e.g., health insurance, pension) are typically available for someone in your profession? I receive 90%—100% paid health and dental. Vision is usually offered at some level. Ours is like $150 year.

What are the key skills necessary for you to succeed in your career? Ability to adapt as needed, get along with others, accept all backgrounds and experiences of others, and to have patience.

Thinking back to your undergraduate career, what courses would you recommend that you believe are key to success in your type of career? Counseling and listening techniques, methods of self-care/relation, cultural competency.

What advice would you give to someone who was thinking about entering the field you are in? Find something you are interested in and follow it. Also, find a program that works for you—small classes if you are shy or want more interactive learning, and so forth.

If you were choosing a career and occupation all over again, what (if anything) would you do differently? No such thing as regrets; I can't think this way.

In thinking about your current career, which of the following categories would you place your career in? Social

In thinking about you and the way you prefer to interact with the world, which of the following categories would you place yourself in? Social

Phoenix provides a great example of someone who pursued additional training, but not to the extent that it required an additional degree. She received training in domestic violence counselor training and received certification in California. Phoenix also recommends finding something you are interested in and following it—in other words, find something that you are passionate about and that you are willing to work hard to achieve. Also, Phoenix echoes a sentiment seen earlier about no regrets. I think Phoenix's mention of cultural competency is important—you need to be able to understand others different from you, whether that comes in your everyday experiences or perhaps from a diversity requirement at your undergraduate institution.

WITH EXPERIENCE COMES RESPONSIBILITY

Your name: Jennifer B.
Your age: 35
Your gender: Female
Your primary job title: Director of operations
Your current employer: Creative Community Options
How long have you been employed in your present position? 1 month
What year did you graduate with your bachelor's degree in psychology? 1994
Describe your major job duties and responsibilities. Operate a community-based residential program for adults with intellectual and developmental disabilities, as well as chronic mental illness. Also operate a supported employment program for the same population groups. Both programs provide support to approximately 140 to 150 individuals. The operations involve overseeing 10 to 12 coordinators who complete the program planning and provide direct supervision to the direct support professionals. That oversight includes managing service rates, contracts, ensuring programs are operating within the state and federal regulations, providing support to the coordinators with challenging staff issues as well as concerns with the individuals we provide support to. There is also significant involvement with the budgeting process of the organization, working to develop and maintain relationships with stakeholders of the organization and assisting in team meetings when there are significant challenges in providing service to an individual.

What elements of your undergraduate training in psychology do you use in your work? In my current position, one of the programs provides services to individuals with chronic mental illness. My degree is helpful in providing support to the coordinator of those individuals. Many of the intellectually disabled individuals also have varying degrees of mental illness. The oversight, both directly and indirectly, of 170-plus employees requires regular use of the training I received in my undergraduate work as well.

What do you like most about your job? I have been in the human service field since leaving undergraduate school. I have always worked with individuals who have some form of a disability. I have a strong passion to see that individuals with intellectual disabilities are given the same opportunities in their life as those without. I get to support the individuals we serve, through the administration of our programs, in living their life as they want to in their own homes or apartments and in jobs at businesses in their own community. Through my experiences as a direct support professional, program manager/coordinator, and Medicaid case manager, I can now develop current coordinators and assist them in learning new skills [with] which [they] will provide the highest of quality of service to the individuals who receive support from our agency.

What do you like least about your job? In this field, there are many regulations, both federal and through our state, that impact the job that we do daily. I feel the regulations are necessary, due to past injustices our field allowed to occur. However, many times the regulations go too far and impact the quality of service as we must focus on items that don't directly impact the people we serve. I now have a strong desire to begin to work with legislators and representatives in an effort to impact the laws and regulations surrounding this field.

Beyond your bachelor's degree, what additional education and/or specialized training have you received? Various training regarding the support of individuals with autism: [Treatment and Education of Autistic and related Communication-handicapped CHildren], [Picture Exchange Communication System], Training in Positive Behavior Support, Mandt, many conferences on supervision of employees.

What is the compensation package for an entry-level position in your occupation? $28,000 to $34,000 salary for a coordinator or case manager. $9 to $11/hour for direct support staff.

What benefits (e.g., health insurance, pension) are typically available for someone in your profession? Health insurance with dental and vision in many places, 401(k), holidays off—unless you are working as a direct support professional. Vacation, sick time, or personal time off. Emergency leave time, flexible hours.

What are the key skills necessary for you to succeed in your career? Passion for the individuals served; organization skills; ability to manage large amounts of paperwork, tight deadlines, and time to handle immediate person-served needs. Soft skills—working well with people, developing resources and information, teaching as opposed to counseling.

Thinking back to your undergraduate career, what courses would you recommend that you believe are key to success in your type of career? Social work courses would have been very helpful to me. I had to learn how to develop assessments on the job and didn't get that in a psychology degree. The assessments in the human service field are looking at the main life domains—where you live, work, your finance situation, social life, spiritual life, and so forth. Classes to learn how to develop a thorough social history and how to work with parents, guardians, or family to get that delicate information. For my current place in my career, management classes are key.

Thinking back to your undergraduate career, can you think of outside of class activities (e.g., research assistantships, internships, Psi Chi) that were key to success in your type of career? My degree in psychology did not require an internship as the social work degree did. I firmly believe that there should be an internship requirement for a psychology degree. Getting out during undergraduate work and obtaining an entry-level position that doesn't require a degree is a great way to start to gain experience as well as to identify what field you want to work in. Psychology is a rather general degree at this point, which is a great cornerstone to further graduate work but is starting to be difficult to use in the human service field. If I were to graduate now with my psychology degree, I would have a difficult time getting to this level in my field. Many positions are requiring a social work license. I am fortunate that the state of Iowa doesn't require it as often as many states do at this time.

As an undergraduate, do you wish you had done anything differently? If so, what? I would have kept my study in psychology and sociology; however, I would have at least minored, if not had a triple major, in social work. That would allow me to now obtain my social work license.

What advice would you give to someone who was thinking about entering the field you are in? Obtain a job with an organization that provides services to individuals with a disability. Get a direct support job, and learn the field directly with the individuals we support. They are your greatest teachers and will help establish the passion for what we do. Many of the positions in my field require that you have at least a year or 2 of direct support experience. It is crucial. Attempt to vary the disability ranges. It is best to have experience with individuals who have a brain injury, individuals with an intellectual disability, and individuals with a chronic mental illness. Substance abuse is also an area of this field that it is helpful to have experience with.

If you were choosing a career and occupation all over again, what (if anything) would you do differently? Absolutely nothing. I am very fortunate to be where I am at in my career at this time. Every position I have had has given me critical experience and information that has allowed me to develop to this place in my professional life.

In thinking about your current career, which of the following categories would you place your career in? Social

In thinking about you and the way you prefer to interact with the world, which of the following categories would you place yourself in? Social

After reading Jennifer's thoughtful comments on the interview questions, I wondered whether she should have written this book! Her advice is too important to skip over. I'll highlight the key points here, but Jennifer's advice is valuable in her own words. First, with some experience after her degree (14-plus years), she moved into a management role as director of operations. Second, her psychology training is useful not only in helping those with disabilities but also in managing her staff of more than 170 employees. Third, the longer Jennifer works in the system, the better she can see the problems to be solved, which explains her interest in working with legislators to help solve these macro-level problems. Fourth, Jennifer sees experience as the key to success, indicating that she wishes an internship had been required as an undergraduate (even if your school does not require an internship, you can still reap the benefits by using your elective credits to complete an internship). Last, as others have suggested with regard to other disciplines and majors, Jennifer would have minored in social work or perhaps even triple-majored in psychology, sociology, and social work.

EMPATHY IS VITAL

Your name: Sherrie M.
Your age: 38
Your gender: Female
Your primary job title: Residential counselor
Your current employer: Luke-Dorf, Inc.
How long have you been employed in your present position? 4 months
What year did you graduate with your bachelor's degree in psychology? 2007
Describe your major job duties and responsibilities. Supervision of 10 mentally ill residential clients in a secure facility, cofacilitate treatment groups, administer psychotropic and other medications to clients, maintain a safe and secure facility.

What elements of your undergraduate training in psychology do you use in your work? This position has been a crash course in abnormal psychology. Our clients have spent anywhere from 5 to 13 years in the state mental hospital and were released into our custody in mid-July of this year. Eight of our 10 clients are under [Psychiatric Security Review Board] and have specific conditions attached to their release (such as attending treatment groups and drug screenings). The clients are stable but severely disabled by their mental illnesses. Typically we are seeing schizophrenia, schizoaffective, bipolar, and other delusional disorders. Most of our clients are also borderline intellectual functioning, which adds another dimension to their care and treatment.

What do you like most about your job? I like working with the clients and learning the practical side of mental illness. You really cannot understand what a hallucination or delusion is until you experience firsthand someone displaying these symptoms. Textbooks cannot capture the reality of mental illnesses and the effect they have on a person's life and ability to function.

What do you like least about your job? The low level of compensation in this industry. I am currently making just $12/hour. This salary is at the high end of the spectrum because of being located in a secure (locked) facility and the criminal backgrounds of our clients. Other facilities pay about $3/hour less.

Beyond your bachelor's degree, what additional education and/or specialized training have you received? I have not received any additional education beyond my BS.

What is the compensation package for an entry-level position in your occupation? Most similar facilities will pay about $9/hour for entry level, but these are not secure. The facility that I work in is the only one of its kind in the area.

What benefits (e.g., health insurance, pension) are typically available for someone in your profession? The agency offers health and dental insurance at a reasonable cost to employees.

What are the key skills necessary for you to succeed in your career? Empathy is vital in this career. If you cannot relate to the clients, it would be very easy to take advantage of their disability and abuse the power you have over them.

Thinking back to your undergraduate career, what courses would you recommend that you believe are key to success in your type of career? A greater understanding of the connection between mental illness and drug abuse would be very helpful. The majority of our clients struggle with both their mental illness and addictions to drugs and alcohol.

Thinking back to your undergraduate career, can you think of outside of class activities (e.g., research assistantships, internships, Psi Chi) that were key to success in your type of career? During my senior year, I worked part time for a residential youth treatment facility that gave me an introduction to working with the mentally ill population.

As an undergraduate, do you wish you had done anything differently? If so, what? I do wish that I had been able to work an internship (I was unable to because of a physical illness).

What advice would you give to someone who was thinking about entering the field you are in? Do your research on the job market and understand that this is not a field in which you will be making a large salary. Many (if not most) of the agencies providing services to this population are nonprofit and do not have the funds to adequately compensate their employees.

If you were choosing a career and occupation all over again, what (if anything) would you do differently? I am still planning on applying

Question to Think About: Have you thought about working at a job during college that can help you explore long-term career opportunities?

to grad school. I know that this is necessary to further my career in helping this underserved population.

In thinking about your current career, which of the following categories would you place your career in? Social

In thinking about you and the way you prefer to interact with the world, which of the following categories would you place yourself in? Social

I really like this quote from Sherrie: "You really cannot understand what a hallucination or delusion is until you experience firsthand someone displaying these symptoms. Textbooks cannot capture the reality of mental illnesses and the effect they have on a person's life and ability to function." Sherrie mentions, as have others with similar workplaces, the necessity for empathy in working with those who are mentally ill. Finally, she recommends (as many others have) the importance of completing an internship.

CLASSROOM CONCEPTS IN REAL LIFE

Your name: Tim H.
Your age: 39
Your gender: Male
Your primary job title: Chief operating officer
Your current employer: Rabiner Treatment Center
How long have you been employed in your present position? 8 years
What year did you graduate with your bachelor's degree in psychology? 1999
Describe your major job duties and responsibilities.

- Responsible for all daily operations of our facility.
- Oversee and guide all programs in our continuum of services, including family-centered services, day treatment services, residential services, and weekend programming.
- Facilitate weekly management meetings with other top management personnel.
- Research and develop new service options for the agency to pursue.
- Responsible for ensuring agency compliance with all regulatory bodies, including certification, purchase of service contracts, Department of Inspection and Appeals, and others.
- Assist in marketing and fund raising for agency needs.

What elements of your undergraduate training in psychology do you use in your work? Dealing with employee motivation and relationships.

What do you like most about your job? Challenge of dealing with delinquent and mentally ill clients.

What do you like least about your job? Dealing with "normal" adult employees who are supposed to follow rules and training, but don't.

Beyond your bachelor's degree, what additional education and/or specialized training have you received? Currently pursuing my MSW at University of Iowa.

What is the compensation package for an entry-level position in your occupation? I currently make $50,000 plus benefits.

What benefits (e.g., health insurance, pension) are typically available for someone in your profession? Health insurance, dental, paid time off.

What are the key skills necessary for you to succeed in your career? Communication skills, problem-solving skills.

Thinking back to your undergraduate career, what courses would you recommend that you believe are key to success in your type of career? I think almost all my psychology courses were very helpful. I could have taken a few more courses in business and workforce strategies.

Thinking back to your undergraduate career, can you think of outside of class activities (e.g., research assistantships, internships, Psi Chi) that were key to success in your type of career? Just working in the human services field has been the best learning experience outside of the classroom for me.

As an undergraduate, do you wish you had done anything differently? If so, what? More courses in business, perhaps.

What advice would you give to someone who was thinking about entering the field you are in? Work in the field as well. You get to see the classroom concepts in real life this way.

If you were choosing a career and occupation all over again, what (if anything) would you do differently? I love what I do, but traditionally the helping fields don't pay well compared with business, and so forth. You have to love this work because the money is not that great.

In thinking about your current career, which of the following categories would you place your career in? Social

In thinking about you and the way you prefer to interact with the world, which of the following categories would you place yourself in? Enterprising

I've included Tim in this book along with a few others who do not currently have a graduate degree but are working on it. Tim echoes a sentiment heard before, that you need to love the work of helping people because the money is not that great. Tim also mentions (twice) that more courses in business would be helpful.

DEVELOP YOUR LEADERSHIP SKILLS

Your name: Nikki W.

Your age: 40

Your gender: Female

Your primary job title: [Qualified mental retardation professional]

Your current employer: Village Northwest Unlimited

How long have you been employed in your present position? 3-plus years in present position.

What year did you graduate with your bachelor's degree in psychology? 1989

Describe your major job duties and responsibilities. I oversee the caseload (vocational, residential, and therapeutic) for people with diagnoses such as mental retardation, autism, cerebral palsy, and so forth. They all require 24-hour supervision and are living in an [intermediate care facility for the mentally retarded] level of care.

What elements of your undergraduate training in psychology do you use in your work? I took several undergrad courses specific to psychology and [mental retardation], so those classes were most helpful. All courses having to do with behavior modification were extremely beneficial.

What do you like most about your job? The flexibility of my hours. I definitely feel like the job I do has a positive impact on the lives of others.

What do you like least about your job? High stress—I'm on call a lot and have to supervise about 40 staff.

Beyond your bachelor's degree, what additional education and/or specialized training have you received? None specific to psychology. I have gone to a lot of training that is job related.

What is the compensation package for an entry-level position in your occupation? I have no idea anymore. I've been in this field for more than 15 years. I will say, don't plan to get rich by working in the social services field!

What benefits (e.g., health insurance, pension) are typically available for someone in your profession? Health insurance, 401(k) equivalent, generous personal and sick time benefits. Because of the typically low pay in social services, many agencies try to find creative ways to offer incentives to their employees (discounts at local businesses, discounts to local attractions—circus tickets, etc.).

What are the key skills necessary for you to succeed in your career? Excellent communication skills, organization, and leadership.

Thinking back to your undergraduate career, what courses would you recommend that you believe are key to success in your type of career? Take whatever opportunities you can to develop leadership skills and work with others in teams. I never work alone—it's always as one part of an interdisciplinary team.

Thinking back to your undergraduate career, can you think of outside of class activities (e.g., research assistantships, internships, Psi Chi) that were key to success in your type of career? I was a [resident assistant] in the dorms and a resident hall director as a senior. Those opportunities to lead probably helped me more in my career than most of my classes!

As an undergraduate, do you wish you had done anything differently? If so, what? I don't really have any regrets. If I could go back, knowing then what I know now, I would have tried to stretch myself a little more academically. I knew from the time I was a sophomore in high school that I would major in psych, but there are so many other things to explore while you are in college. I wish I had had a wider focus.

What advice would you give to someone who was thinking about entering the field you are in? People often enter the world of social services with the idea that they will work for a year or two and then move on. Beware that

Question to Think About: If you were in a management position in the health care field, how would you deal with the stress of supervising employees in addition to the stressors of the types of clients you may serve?

you will likely never move on! Serving others, if that is your purpose in life, is addictive. There is no better way to put service above self than to advocate for people who are unable to advocate for themselves.

If you were choosing a career and occupation all over again, what (if anything) would you do differently? I started out in TBI [traumatic brain injury] rehabilitation. If I had it to do all over again, I would have stayed the course with that specialty and not taken various promotions that ultimately led more into serving people with mental retardation, autism, cerebral palsy, etc. Along those lines, I would probably have explored emergency medicine—not to practice but to be able to understand the TBI rehab side of things better.

In thinking about your current career, which of the following categories would you place your career in? Social

In thinking about you and the way you prefer to interact with the world, which of the following categories would you place yourself in? Social

Nikki offers some advice we have heard before, but also some new insights. She reminds us that one does not get rich working in the social services field, but also that she has no regrets (again, themes we've heard before). But when thinking back to her undergraduate career, Nikki believes that her experiences as a resident assistant and residence hall director were probably more influential to her than most of her classes. Often it is an outside-of-class experience, such as serving as a resident assistant, intern, or Psi Chi officer, that can provide an insightful experience to an undergraduate student. Do not underestimate the importance and potential impact of these experiences.

UNDERGRADUATE RESEARCH PROJECTS ARE HELPFUL

Your name: Shelley D.

Your age: 46

Your gender: Female

Your primary job title: Residential care facility administrator

Your current employer: Hope Haven Area Development Center Corporation

How long have you been employed in your present position? 3 months

What year did you graduate with your bachelor's degree in psychology? 1983

Describe your major job duties and responsibilities. I oversee a 15-bed residential care facility. This includes supervising a staff of 14, being responsible for the budget of the facility, making sure all policies and procedures are followed according to local, state, and national guidelines.

What elements of your undergraduate training in psychology do you use in your work? Frequently look at diagnosis and medications. Have to be aware of what medications are used for what mental illnesses, what symptoms of various mental illnesses are, and how to interpret IQ testing.

What do you like most about your job? I enjoy working with the residents and assisting them in obtaining various skills to reach their potential.

What do you like least about your job? The constantly changing regulations.

Beyond your bachelor's degree, what additional education and/or specialized training have you received? I have ongoing training through our organization. This includes CPR and first aid, adult abuse reporting, various leadership and supervisory training, employment specialist training.

What is the compensation package for an entry-level position in your occupation? We offer health and dental insurance as well as paid life insurance. We have a retirement program in which Hope Haven will provide matching funds up to 3% of your annual salary. We also offer paid sick, vacation, and casual days.

What benefits (e.g., health insurance, pension) are typically available for someone in your profession? These are generally the common and standard benefits available in this area to entry-level positions in this field.

What are the key skills necessary for you to succeed in your career? Being good with people; good communication skills, both verbal and written; ability to use good judgment; be a self starter; good organization skills; good typing skills; and flexibility.

Thinking back to your undergraduate career, what courses would you recommend that you believe are key to success in your type of career? Abnormal psychology and some type of pharmaceutical course. Because of the wide variety of people whom I interact with, I think a variety of courses are important, including child development courses.

Thinking back to your undergraduate career, can you think of outside of class activities (e.g., research assistantships, internships, Psi Chi) that were key to success in your type of career? We had to complete a variety of research projects that students had to be involved in. I think those were especially helpful. Any internship in a facility would be beneficial.

What advice would you give to someone who was thinking about entering the field you are in? You are not going to become independently wealthy; however, the intrinsic value of the job and knowing that you are helping to better someone's life is a great responsibility and reward.

If you were choosing a career and occupation all over again, what (if anything) would you do differently? Probably go on to get a master's degree in counseling.

In thinking about your current career, which of the following categories would you place your career in? Social

In thinking about you and the way you prefer to interact with the world, which of the following categories would you place yourself in? Social

I think Shelley is right on target when she describes the key skills necessary for a successful career: "Being good with people; good communication skills, both verbal and written; ability to use good judgment; be a self starter; good organization skills; good typing skills; and flexibility." Personally, I like that she mentioned typing skills. I have often thought that my typing class was the most important class I took in high school! Shelley poignantly demonstrates, as others have as well, what the true rewards are in working in this type of field: "You are not going to become independently wealthy; however, the intrinsic value of the job and knowing that you are helping to better someone's life is a great responsibility and reward." If you find yourself agreeing with these types of statements, working in one of the many health care professions may be for you.

DEDICATION TO THOSE YOU ARE HELPING

Your name: James K.
Your age: 47
Your gender: Male
Your primary job title: Codirector of community living
Your current employer: Village Northwest Unlimited
How long have you been employed in your present position? 27 years
What year did you graduate with your bachelor's degree in psychology? 1982
Describe your major job duties and responsibilities. I am responsible for coordinating services for nearly 60 clients. Our clients are all adults with physical or mental disabilities or both. I also help oversee the 60 staff who provide care and services for these individuals, including meeting with them on a quarterly basis to review the care programs being provided and conducting performance reviews. I help develop new training goals, and provide guidance to staff and clients on how to effectively complete their work and grow. I conduct quality assurance on documentation samples that are written by our staff and perform follow-up reports to the various staff teams that we supervise. One of our goals is to encourage and support our staff, and we make this a priority in our work.

What elements of your undergraduate training in psychology do you use in your work? I would say the training we received in counseling and helping techniques is probably the most beneficial and frequently used education from my undergraduate training.

What do you like most about your job? The flexibility of schedule.

What do you like least about your job? Bureaucracy and poor communication with and from the various funding streams that we work with and those hired to oversee this. Poor wages for staff.

What is the compensation package for an entry-level position in your occupation? It would be a range of $19,000 to 25,000 for a middle management person, $15,000 to $18,000 for a full-time direct care staff.

What benefits (e.g., health insurance, pension) are typically available for someone in your profession? Major medical health insurance, life insurance, various perks offered by our agency such as reduced costs for various items like newspaper subscriptions, wellness or fitness memberships.

What are the key skills necessary for you to succeed in your career? Patience, good listening abilities, creativity, understanding, integrity, honesty, and willingness to go the extra mile.

Thinking back to your undergraduate career, what courses would you recommend that you believe are key to success in your type of career? Abnormal psychology, theories of counseling, developmental psychology.

As an undergraduate, do you wish you had done anything differently? If so, what? I don't think so; I was adequately prepared in my education for my job.

What advice would you give to someone who was thinking about entering the field you are in? Be focused and dedicated to the people you are serving or trying to help. They are someone else's son or daughter and have tremendous value. Try to instill ways of making your job fun and enjoyable. Encourage and support those who work with you. Create a climate of participative decision making so that everyone feels invested in what is being decided. Show honor and respect to those above you and to those you come into contact with each day; make them feel valued and important.

If you were choosing a career and occupation all over again, what (if anything) would you do differently? I can't think of anything that I would choose to do differently.

In thinking about your current career, which of the following categories would you place your career in? Social

In thinking about you and the way you prefer to interact with the world, which of the following categories would you place yourself in? Social

James provides another example of someone who works with adults with physical or mental disabilities. His advice on how to help others clearly comes from the perspective of someone who is used to being exposed to those who experience the effects of mental illness: "Be focused and dedicated to the people you are serving or trying to help. They are someone else's son or daughter and have tremendous value." Thinking about your clients as someone else's son or daughter would certainly help to keep you grounded in this work environment.

POLITICS AND FUNDING SERVICES

Your name: Catherine M.
Your age: 50
Your gender: Female

The name of your professional association? Iowa Association of Community Providers

Your primary job title: Community living director

Your current employer: Genesis Development

How long have you been employed in your present position? 18 years

What year did you graduate with your bachelor's degree in psychology? 1980

Describe your major job duties and responsibilities. Program development; hiring, training, supervising staff; development of policy, programs, budgets.

What elements of your undergraduate training in psychology do you use in your work? I received a good general overview—I find that there are many areas to go into under the heading of psychology and that once entering a "specialty" area, most do their own training particular to that field. This one is the same—and I have actually written staff training programs for this field, as there is very little out there.

What do you like most about your job? Being creative and responsive to the people who show up at "our door" looking for supports and services. The challenge is to (a) find a way to develop and provide those services as needed and (b) get those supports funded. The most significant thing to me is that we do change the course of people's lives for the better; those who would otherwise in all likelihood never know a life with any dignity, productivity, or options.

What do you like least about your job? The periodic bureaucracy/politics involved in keeping the funding streams available and viable so people can get what they need in the way of services.

Beyond your bachelor's degree, what additional education and/or specialized training have you received? Many shorter term trainings, mostly from two areas: (a) more detailed information regarding the particular types of disabilities I have worked with and (b) training in supervision and management, particularly working with managing a budget, grant writing, and so forth.

What is the compensation package for an entry-level position in your occupation? Typically salaried positions; they vary a great deal from state to state and whether or not they are private or government positions. I would generalize and say very comparable to teaching positions in most areas.

What benefits (e.g., health insurance, pension) are typically available for someone in your profession? In the private sector, it is common to be offered medical coverage, vacation/sick leave, and various other insurance coverages; benefits like having access to an [employee assistance] program are often available. Some offer a retirement package, many don't. In most states, there are significant differences between government job wages and those available in the private sector.

What are the key skills necessary for you to succeed in your career? A lot of flexibility; ability to change with the policies and funding issues within

Question to Think About: Do you have a more specific goal than "I want to help people?"

whatever the current political climate is. Most staff continue to develop in one of two directions: supervisory and management skills or they go on to graduate training to specialize in a more therapeutic position.

Thinking back to your undergraduate career, what courses would you recommend that you believe are key to success in your type of career? I can't think back that far. But, in some regard they were all so general that they did not specifically prepare you for any particular area of service.

Thinking back to your undergraduate career, can you think of outside of class activities (e.g., research assistantships, internships, Psi Chi) that were key to success in your type of career? More actual experience in various types of positions I believe would be the most helpful thing to do. I found it is tremendously different to study psychology [than to work] in the field. The various stresses and things that impact you are quite different depending on the area of service that you work in, and it would be extremely helpful to have some hands-on experience trying out numerous arenas to help find where you best fit, and where your interests and talents really lie.

As an undergraduate, do you wish you had done anything differently? If so, what? More specific information about the various fields, what the actual positions would be like, and what career development would look like depending on the same.

What advice would you give to someone who was thinking about entering the field you are in? Try out being in the environment first—volunteer, work part time, take a direct line position. Spend time meeting, talking with, interviewing people currently in the field you feel you are interested in to get a better overall feel for what that is like on a day-to-day basis. Just having a sense of "I want to help people" will not be enough direction to focus your efforts, or have a realistic idea of what skills and temperament fit better in various jobs.

If you were choosing a career and occupation all over again, what (if anything) would you do differently? I would have spent more time looking at the big picture involved with the field, pluses and minuses of different areas and made a choice that was perhaps more inclusive of more factors than what I initially looked at.

In thinking about your current career, which of the following categories would you place your career in? Social

In thinking about you and the way you prefer to interact with the world, which of the following categories would you place yourself in? Social

As Catherine advances in her career, she deals more and more with bureaucracy and politics—which usually accompany more supervisory responsibility. Catherine puts into words the real rewards for those who help others lead a more fulfilling life: "The most significant thing to me is that we do change the course of people's lives for the better; those who would otherwise in all likelihood never know a life with any dignity, productivity, or options." She also points out that the book knowledge that she learned as an undergraduate differs from what she sees in the field. Catherine also echoes the advice of others who suggest that undergraduates check out the world of work before graduating by volunteering, working part time, or, as many have suggested, participating in an internship. Her advice about focus is exactly on target: "Just having a sense of 'I want to help people' will not be enough direction."

I divided the interviewees who fell into the social category by age and presented this information across two chapters. In the next chapter, I present the results of the interviews in which baccalaureates self-identified as enterprising—the second most frequent category that respondents listed.

Enterprising Careers   5

G iven its close association with the field of psychology, it is not overly surprising that the social category of Holland code occupations was the most frequently reported. What is surprising is that the second most popular category was *enterprising*—the topic of this chapter.

Descriptions and Sample Occupations

In Holland's (1994) Self-Directed Search,

> Enterprising (E) people like enterprising careers such as buyer, sports promoter, television producer, business executive, salesperson, travel agent, supervisor, and manager. The E type usually has leadership and public speaking abilities, is interested in money and politics, and likes to influence people. The E type generally likes to persuade or direct others more than work on scientific or complicated topics. The E type is described as acquisitive, adventurous, agreeable, ambitious, attention-getting, domineering, energetic, extroverted, impulsive, optimistic, pleasure-seeking, popular, self-confident, and sociable. (Reardon, n.d., ¶8)

Interviews

In all, six individuals completing the online survey self-identified as enterprising. Their interview results are presented below.

MANAGING CLINICAL TRIALS

Your name: Dayna G.

Your age: 25

Your gender: Female

Your primary job title: Clinical affairs project manager

Your current employer: Third Wave Technologies

How long have you been employed in your present position? 7 months

What year did you graduate with your bachelor's degree in psychology? 2003

Describe your major job duties and responsibilities. Managing clinical trial activities for molecular diagnostic products. Coordinating efforts between the clinical sites, contract research organizations, and trial vendors on a day-to-day basis.

What elements of your undergraduate training in psychology do you use in your work? Classes such as statistical methods, research methods, biological psychiatry, and analyzing psychological research have prepared me for designing clinical trials, developing my critical thinking skills, and understanding and writing journal articles in peer-reviewed journals.

What do you like most about your job? The diverse amount of projects and being able to work with a multitude of professionals in the clinical trial industry.

Beyond your bachelor's degree, what additional education and/or specialized training have you received? I have completed six training courses in project management related to MS project, managing clinical trials, and leadership and development.

What is the compensation package for an entry-level position in your occupation? Varies by location and industry (pharmaceutical, diagnostic, [contract research organization]). Anywhere from $40,000 to $60,000.

What benefits (e.g., health insurance, pension) are typically available for someone in your profession? Full health and dental, 401(k), stock options, 2 to 3 weeks paid vacation and personal time, flexible schedule, paid training, life insurance.

What are the key skills necessary for you to succeed in your career? Flexibility, time management, ability to communicate effectively in both small and large team environments, assertiveness, ability to take initiative/ motivation.

Question to Think About: Think about your least favorite classes. In what ways might you be able to use what you have learned in them?

Thinking back to your undergraduate career, what courses would you recommend that you believe are key to success in your type of career? Research methods, statistical methods, biology/genetics.

Thinking back to your undergraduate career, can you think of outside of class activities (e.g., research assistantships, internships, Psi Chi) that were key to success in your type of career? Research assistantships with professors, presenting research at Psi Chi and other conferences, [being] president of Psychology Club.

As an undergraduate, do you wish you had done anything differently? If so, what? Spoke with different types of professionals in other fields besides psychology. There are many other fields related to psychology that can be a perfect fit for a psychology major.

What advice would you give to someone who was thinking about entering the field you are in? Ensure you have a diverse background and take several science courses. The pharmaceutical industry and biotech industry are growing exponentially, and just a few science courses can help you get a foot in the door.

If you were choosing a career and occupation all over again, what (if anything) would you do differently? Complete [more] science courses such as genetics and advanced biology.

In thinking about your current career, which of the following categories would you place your career in? Enterprising

In thinking about you and the way you prefer to interact with the world, which of the following categories would you place yourself in? Social

One of the items that Dayna mentions right away that caught my attention is her emphasis on methodology courses, such as statistics, research methods, biology, and so forth. She also acknowledges that experiences outside the classroom, such as serving as a research assistant or as president of Psychology Club, were keys to her successful career. Writing journal articles was also an important skill for Dayna to master.

WORK ETHIC LEADS TO PAYOFF

Your name: Steve S.
Your age: 37
Your gender: Male
Your primary job title: President and CEO
Your current employer: Solera Networks
How long have you been employed in your present position? 10 months
What year did you graduate with your bachelor's degree in psychology? 1992

Describe your major job duties and responsibilities. Responsible for the day-to-day operations and strategic positioning for a high-tech startup.

What elements of your undergraduate training in psychology do you use in your work?

- Interpersonal relationship skills
- Pattern recognition
- Positive and negative reinforcement techniques

What do you like most about your job? Each day presents a new and unique set of challenges. I enjoy rallying a team of smart people around a goal and driving the company to achieve that goal.

What do you like least about your job? "Administrivia"—I really dislike the tactical administration aspects; things that most of us take for granted in larger corporations.

Beyond your bachelor's degree, what additional education and/or specialized training have you received? Two years of graduate school in psychology.

What is the compensation package for an entry-level position in your occupation? In a CEO position for a startup, one should expect a lower minimum salary and more equity. Base salaries are quite varied, but something starting in the $150K range seems reasonable.

What benefits (e.g., health insurance, pension) are typically available for someone in your profession? Health, dental, and life are typical. In a startup, one should not expect a 401(k); rather, company equity is more common.

What are the key skills necessary for you to succeed in your career?

- Work ethic—being willing to put in the hours to ensure success
- Attention to detail
- Good pattern recognition and interpersonal skills

Thinking back to your undergraduate career, what courses would you recommend that you believe are key to success in your type of career? Intro to learning statistics, social psychology.

Thinking back to your undergraduate career, can you think of outside of class activities (e.g., research assistantships, internships, Psi Chi) that were key to success in your type of career? Working in Hal Miller's lab was a great experience. Acting as a manager of the operation gave me great experience in handling budgets, people, and projects. Looking back, this may have provided the single most salient experience that could be directly applied to my current position.

As an undergraduate, do you wish you had done anything differently? If so, what? I would have changed my minor to be more practical (from analytic philosophy to economics). I may have focused more on applied psychology versus basic research.

Question to Think About: How would you feel about trying to become more involved outside the classroom, such as being a research assistant?

What advice would you give to someone who was thinking about entering the field you are in? Be prepared to work hard, face seemingly insurmountable obstacles with zeal, and otherwise be presented with daunting challenges. The payoff is satisfaction in growing something from nothing, and making a mark in your representative industry. Ultimately, if one is successful, financial reward will follow.

If you were choosing a career and occupation all over again, what (if anything) would you do differently? I might have gone on to law school instead of graduate school, but I ultimately enjoy what I am doing now very much.

In thinking about your current career, which of the following categories would you place your career in? Enterprising

In thinking about you and the way you prefer to interact with the world, which of the following categories would you place yourself in? Artistic

First, I like Steve's labeling of *administrivia*—the types of tasks that involve planning and maintenance in larger organizations. These would be items such as budget meetings, developing promotion standards, designing security systems, and so forth. Second, Steve acknowledges that being in charge of a professor's laboratory while in school may have been the single most influential experience in helping him to achieve what he has achieved. Finally, he provides words of inspiration for us all: "Be prepared to work hard, face seemingly insurmountable obstacles with zeal, and otherwise be presented with daunting challenges. The payoff is satisfaction in growing something from nothing."

SEEING PROGRESS DAILY

Your name: Michael M.

Your age: 38

Your gender: Male

Your primary job title: General contractor

Your current employer: Self-employed

How long have you been employed in your present position? 5 years

What year did you graduate with your bachelor's degree in psychology? 1993

Describe your major job duties and responsibilities. Organizing aspects of fine custom home building. We build houses more than 5,000 square feet. My company handles fine carpentry and woodworking.

What elements of your undergraduate training in psychology do you use in your work? I get some of America's best and brightest to do what I want them to as construction workers. I also get those who owe me money to pay it. You must size up a person and speak accordingly to get results.

What do you like most about your job? Constant change of working environment, by physical location, and seeing progress daily.

What do you like least about your job? Giving people bad news. Construction always takes longer and costs more.

Beyond your bachelor's degree, what additional education and/or specialized training have you received? Working in construction for too long while waiting to develop desire to go back to school for graduate work.

What is the compensation package for an entry-level position in your occupation? $10 per hour as a carpenter.

What benefits (e.g., health insurance, pension) are typically available for someone in your profession? Whatever the self-employed can eke out.

What are the key skills necessary for you to succeed in your career? Endeavor to persevere, thrive on stress, never give up.

Thinking back to your undergraduate career, what courses would you recommend that you believe are key to the success in your type of career? Philosophy double major was very important.

What advice would you give to someone who was thinking about entering the field you are in? Do related class work.

In thinking about your current career, which of the following categories would you place your career in? Enterprising

In thinking about you and the way you prefer to interact with the world, which of the following categories would you place yourself in? Enterprising

Michael speaks to the positives (seeing progress daily) and the negatives (getting people to pay when they owe money) of the construction industry and being self-employed. Also, he emphasizes a combination of interests that you wouldn't expect; self-employment in the construction industry and the importance of his double major in philosophy and psychology. Sometimes, you just don't know where your path will lead you—a course that may seem silly or irrelevant at the time may have a payoff in the long run. You just don't know.

BUILDING CONFIDENCE IN PUBLIC

Your name: Melissa S.

Your age: 40

Your gender: Female

Your primary job title: Associate manager

Your current employer: American Diabetes Association

How long have you been employed in your present position? 1½ years

What year did you graduate with your bachelor's degree in psychology? 1988

Describe your major job duties and responsibilities. Fundraiser; responsible for all logistics, sponsorships, and dollars raised for Baltimore Step Out to Fight Diabetes walk-a-thon.

> **Question to Think About:** What performance skills do you have or want to develop? How will performance skills help you in the public roles your career might involve?

What elements of your undergraduate training in psychology do you use in your work? Work with many different types of people—[you] need good people skills, and I'm sure the classes I took helped to some degree.

What do you like most about your job? Communication with people—inspiring them to do well and have fun with the fundraising process.

What do you like least about your job? The bureaucratic and political crap involved with being part of a huge agency. Normal day-to-day frustrations also bother me—general office things going wrong—which happens often.

Beyond your bachelor's degree, what additional education and/or specialized training have you received? Professional singer

What is the compensation package for an entry-level position in your occupation? Approximately $37,000 yearly

What benefits (e.g., health insurance, pension) are typically available for someone in your profession? Health insurance, retirement benefits when vested in 3 years, disability, vacation, personal time, sick time, holidays—9 of them.

What are the key skills necessary for you to succeed in your career? Extremely organized, good writing skills, good interpersonal skills, ability to multi-task, following up well, tenacity.

Thinking back to your undergraduate career, what courses would you recommend that you believe are key to success in your type of career? Honestly, I don't even remember what I took and how it helped me with anything in particular.

Thinking back to your undergraduate career, can you think of outside of class activities (e.g., research assistantships, internships, Psi Chi) that were key to success in your type of career? Singing in bands and getting out in front of the public and around the city was very helpful.

As an undergraduate, do you wish you had done anything differently? If so, what? Wish I was a theater or music major and performed in school more.

What advice would you give to someone who was thinking about entering the field you are in? If they are truly interested in pursuing a psych degree and [in] working in the field, I would recommend going on to medical school or master's/PhD level to have any bit of success.

If you were choosing a career and occupation all over again, what (if anything) would you do differently? Choose different major or go on to graduate school right away.

In thinking about your current career, which of the following categories would you place your career in? Enterprising

In thinking about you and the way you prefer to interact with the world, which of the following categories would you place yourself in? Artistic

Melissa brings unique experiences from her background—a singing career—to help with her current career—fundraising. The confidence she developed by singing in public has clearly benefitted her; we saw a similar experience with a former Miss Vermont in chapter 3. Although Melissa found a rewarding line of work, her undergraduate career in psychology is not that memorable, and if she had it to do all over again, she would choose a different major or go directly to graduate school. The reality is that an undergraduate degree in psychology will not fulfill every student completely. For some, it provides a wonderful base from which to build, but others have to rebuild their base. Melissa's story reminds us that we must each make our own path and seek out satisfaction along the way.

THE ABILITY TO MAKE A DIFFERENCE

Your name: Kimberly C.

Your age: 43

Your gender: Female

Your primary job title: Director of marketing and public relations

Your current employer: ResCare, Inc.

How long have you been employed in your present position? 4 years

What year did you graduate with your bachelor's degree in psychology? 1986

Describe your major job duties and responsibilities. I am responsible for marketing the wide array of services my company offers, in coordination with regional administrators and staff. I develop brochures, press releases, newspaper articles, and other advertising. I also sit on the senior management team of my company, allowing me to participate in long-term strategic planning and oversight of my company, which employs more than 600 people. I am particularly involved in business development, which includes researching and involvement in business startup.

What elements of your undergraduate training in psychology do you use in your work? Currently, I use my understanding of psychology to guide employees in our mission, vision, and core values. Relationship issues are valuable in the workplace, and I believe my training in psychology has helped in that area. It helps me to relate to other staff members, including psychiatrists, therapists, and direct support staff in problem solving and looking for growth opportunities. Additionally, my degree in psychology opened the door for me to get into the field of providing services to persons with serious and persistent mental illness and other disabilities. My experience coupled with my education has allowed me to be successful and therefore promotable.

What do you like most about your job? Advocating for persons with disabilities to empower themselves, by influencing the culture of my company.

What do you like least about your job? Government bureaucracy

Beyond your bachelor's degree, what additional education and/or specialized training have you received? A few MBA classes; sales and marketing training when I left the human services field for 6 years to go into the financial services field; countless internal and external training sessions on service provision, leadership, marketing, business administration.

What is the compensation package for an entry-level position in your occupation? A person with a bachelor's degree in psychology could begin at the $28,000–$30,000 per year level. However, direct support staff typically start out at $8–$10 per hour.

What benefits (e.g., health insurance, pension) are typically available for someone in your profession? Health insurance, life insurance, dental insurance, 401(k) with nice match, personal time off, holidays off; and through my employee-owned company, I have stock ownership. As a stockholder, I have long-term care insurance for myself and my spouse with a partial company premium payment.

What are the key skills necessary for you to succeed in your career? Ability to relate well with people, be a reliable team player and leader; have a positive "can-do" attitude. Technical skills include computer skills, writing skills, public relations, and strategic planning skills.

Thinking back to your undergraduate career, what courses would you recommend that you believe are key to success in your type of career? General psychology, abnormal psychology, history of psychology (different schools of thought), speech, literature and creative writing, contemporary social problems, sociology, behavioral psychology.

Thinking back to your undergraduate career, can you think of outside of class activities (e.g., research assistantships, internships, Psi Chi) that were key to success in your type of career? I belonged to the Student Senate and Alpha Phi Omega (a service coed fraternity), but I can't say that either was key to my success.

As an undergraduate, do you wish you had done anything differently? If so, what? I wish I had taken more business-related classes.

What advice would you give to someone who was thinking about entering the field you are in? It's a wonderful and rewarding career. I left it for a period of time and have never regretted coming back. However, don't expect to walk into a high-paying, professional position out of college. Most people will need to get experience working in the field. Opportunities for growth and advancement are available. Hard work and good work ethics will take you far. This is also a good field for those looking for flexibility with an ability to make a difference.

Question to Think About: Under what circumstances would you go back to school? If your career aspirations change? Just because you wanted to go back to school?

If you were choosing a career and occupation all over again, what (if anything) would you do differently? I probably wouldn't do anything differently. My initial plan was to go straight to graduate school to get my master's in psychology after I graduated with my bachelor's. However, that did not work out, and I am glad. I am better suited for a career in health care administration and business management than as a therapist or counselor. I still hope to complete my MBA in the future, but I'm glad I have work experience instead of going immediately to graduate school.

In thinking about your current career, which of the following categories would you place your career in? Enterprising

In thinking about you and the way you prefer to interact with the world, which of the following categories would you place yourself in? Enterprising

Kimberly tells an interesting story. As a director of marketing and public relations, she has been able to use her background in psychology and previous experience working with individuals with mental illness to help her in her career. She, as have others, also recommends more business-related classes. As someone who has risen in the corporate ranks, Kimberly complains (as others have) about the bureaucracy that goes along with added responsibilities. Kimberly is also candid about her initial plans to attend graduate school (like many students); when that didn't work out, she made the best of it. Kimberly acknowledges, too, that she can still attend graduate school in the future, but for her, it will be to obtain an MBA.

HELPING OTHERS REALIZE THEIR POTENTIAL

Your name: Dan Y.
Your age: 55
Your gender: Male
Your primary job title: Executive director
Your current employer: ECHO PLUS Inc.
How long have you been employed in your present position? 30 years
What year did you graduate with your bachelor's degree in psychology? 1973
Describe your major job duties and responsibilities. I am the executive director for a nonprofit agency that serves 150 people who have a mental or physical disability. My duties include public relations, human resources, budgets and fiscal responsibility, policies and procedures, working with our board, staff supervision, and so forth.

What elements of your undergraduate training in psychology do you use in your work? Abnormal psychology and probably just the understanding and compassion that we need to work with the people we serve. My BS in psychology just opened doors for me that allowed me to use my 5 years' previous experience to become the director at age 25.

What do you like most about your job? The challenge that we face in helping people to realize their potential and become successful in meeting their goals in their lives, work, and dreams. When they get to live in their first apartment or find and secure a job that meets their needs, it is great!

What do you like least about your job? The politics involved in funding and sometimes the battles between funding needs and the tightening of funds.

Beyond your bachelor's degree, what additional education and/or specialized training have you received? I took a workshop maybe 25 years ago that was for training rehabilitation administrators through the University of Missouri. Maybe four or five 2-day sessions.

What is the compensation package for an entry-level position in your occupation? Entry level with successful middle management experience, smaller agency: $50,000 with all benefits.

What benefits (e.g., health insurance, pension) are typically available for someone in your profession? Health insurance, 403(b) pension, and so forth.

What are the key skills necessary for you to succeed in your career? Supervise other managers; be able to relate to all kinds of people, react to change in such a way that the people who are part of the organization will buy into it.

Thinking back to your undergraduate career, what courses would you recommend that you believe are key to success in your type of career? Human relations, course on mental illness.

Thinking back to your undergraduate career, can you think of outside of class activities (e.g., research assistantships, internships, Psi Chi) that were key to success in your type of career? Volunteering at a good nonprofit to make a positive impression to get the first job and subsequent experience. Come to think of it, I basically started as a teacher's aide but received a promotion to a coordinator after 6 months.

As an undergraduate, do you wish you had done anything differently? If so, what? I had a minor in education, but my advisor neglected to tell me that there would be no "9 to 12" jobs in teaching psych.

What advice would you give to someone who was thinking about entering the field you are in? I think that many larger agencies may be looking for a master's, but a middle management position might be good in a larger agency. Also, in rural areas the opportunity might still be available to direct a smaller agency like ours.

If you were choosing a career and occupation all over again, what (if anything) would you do differently? I'm pretty happy with the opportunities I've had. From my generation, I always wanted to make a difference in the world. Now I even get paid pretty well to have that opportunity.

In thinking about your current career, which of the following categories would you place your career in? Enterprising

In thinking about you and the way you prefer to interact with the world, which of the following categories would you place yourself in? Social

Dan articulates what he likes about his job, which may be inspiring for the rest of us:

> The challenge that we face helping people to realize their potential and become successful in meeting their goals in their lives, work, and dreams. When they get to live in their first apartment or find and secure a job that meets their needs, it is great!

Dan also mentions the importance of advising, but in a round-about way, by pointing out information that his advisor neglected to tell him. Also, for Dan volunteering yielded future opportunities.

Some of our common themes continue to emerge in this set of interviews: a desire for more background in business and the importance of an abnormal psychology course. In chapter 7, I explore in more depth why these (and other) opportunities are so important. In the next chapter, however, you'll find the interviews from those who identified themselves as conventional, realistic, artistic, or investigative.

Conventional, Realistic, Artistic, and Investigative Careers

6

D ata that are difficult to obtain are for that same reason valuable. My method of data collection for this book necessitated volunteers completing online interviews, and I am grateful for each and every person who completed one. Ideally, I would have obtained equal numbers of social, enterprising, conventional, realistic, artistic, and investigative individuals (or perhaps just a representative sample). Most psychological employment positions are linked to the Holland (1974) social category, and many fall into the enterprising category; however, there are those that fall into the other categories.

In this chapter, I combine the interviews representing the remaining four occupational categories: two interviews for the conventional category, one interview for the realistic category, and one interview for the artistic category.

Descriptions and Sample Occupations

Conventional (C) people like conventional careers such as bookkeeper, financial analyst, banker, tax expert, secretary, and radio dispatcher. The C type has clerical and math abilities, likes to work indoors and to organize things. The C type generally likes to follow orderly routines and meet clear standards, avoiding work that does not have clear directions. The C type is described as conforming, conscientious, careful, efficient, inhibited, obedient, orderly, persistent, practical, thrifty, and unimaginative. (Reardon, n.d., ¶9)

Realistic (R) people like realistic careers such as auto mechanic, aircraft controller, surveyor, electrician, and farmer. The R type usually has mechanical and athletic abilities, and likes to work outdoors and with tools and machines. The R type generally likes to work with things more than with people. The R type is described as conforming, frank, genuine, hardheaded, honest, humble, materialistic, modest, natural, normal, persistent, practical, shy, and thrifty. (Reardon, n.d., ¶4)

Artistic (A) people like artistic careers such as composer, musician, stage director, dancer, interior decorator, actor, and writer. The A type usually has artistic skills, enjoys creating original work, and has a good imagination. The A type generally likes to work with creative ideas and self-expression more than routines and rules. The A type is described as complicated, disorderly, emotional, expressive, idealistic, imaginative, impractical, impulsive, independent, introspective, intuitive, nonconforming, open, and original. (Reardon, n.d., ¶6)

Investigative (I) people like investigative careers such as biologist, chemist, physicist, geologist, anthropologist, laboratory assistant, and medical technician. The I type usually has math and science abilities, and likes to work alone and to solve problems. The I type generally likes to explore and understand things or events, rather than persuade others or sell them things. The I type is described as analytical, cautious, complex, critical, curious, independent, intellectual, introverted, methodical, modest, pessimistic, precise, rational, and reserved. (Reardon, n.d., ¶5)

Interviews

CONVENTIONAL

Statistical Analysis of Survey Data

Your name: Kathy K.
Your age: 24
Your gender: Female
Your primary job title: Statistician and survey analyst
How long have you been employed in your present position? 2½ years
What year did you graduate with your bachelor's degree in psychology? 2005
Describe your major job duties and responsibilities. My organization works in improving employee relations with health care organizations

Question to Think About: Being good at something that others dread (e.g., math or SPSS) can make you very marketable. Think about your skills; what do you enjoy that could be valuable to an employer?

around the country. I spend the majority of my time creating surveys and researching new trends in health care organizations. I help develop questionnaire items that will provide actionable data to our clients. I also analyze the data we receive using statistical methods, and create reports for the surveys.

What elements of your undergraduate training in psychology do you use in your work? A lot of my work uses my research methods experience from college. Other aspects of my work include my statistics classes and my course on psychological assessment. I also developed strong critical thinking skills in my courses and apply those and my training in SPSS on a regular basis.

What do you like most about your job? Working with numbers and finding interesting trends in the numbers that apply to real-world people. Each individual person may not have much of a say in the organization, but it is quite interesting to see that together they can impact how it is structured. I also like to see how certain demographics impact the results.

What do you like least about your job? Trying to explain statistics can be difficult; I get frustrated easily.

What is the compensation package for an entry-level position in your occupation? $38,000 plus an annual bonus up to 12%.

What benefits (e.g., health insurance, pension) are typically available for someone in your profession? Full benefits: health care, dental, vision, life insurance, short-term disability/long-term disability, 401(k), and a whole lot of other things I don't often pay attention to.

What are the key skills necessary for you to succeed in your career? Critical thinking!!! Attention to detail. Basic knowledge of research methods with a focus on survey design.

Thinking back to your undergraduate career, what courses would you recommend that you believe are key to success in your type of career? Research methods, statistics, psychological assessment, performing an external research project.

Thinking back to your undergraduate career, can you think of outside of class activities (e.g., research assistantships, internships, Psi Chi) that were key to success in your type of career? I spent a lot of time in the psychology department; the more you get to know the professors, the more help they can be. Get to know your professors more than just "hi/bye." They can provide you with valuable information, recommendations, and even direct you toward a rewarding career.

As an undergraduate, do you wish you had done anything differently? If so, what? More external research and an advanced statistics course.

What advice would you give to someone who was thinking about entering the field you are in? It is rewarding work that I enjoy. Working for a company that helps improve employee relations means that we have a great culture of trust and a good performance management system. I would definitely recommend it. Really, just find different consulting firms in your area and look into them.

In thinking about your current career, which of the following categories would you place your career in? Conventional

In thinking about you and the way you prefer to interact with the world, which of the following categories would you place yourself in? Investigative

Kathy discusses some of the practical aspects of her job that psychology instructors often emphasize, like the understanding of survey and questionnaire data and the use of SPSS. She also mentions something that I talk about all the time in my classes—attention to detail. Attention to detail often makes the difference between a good student and a great student or, said another way, between a B and an A. Kathy's advice regarding getting to know your psychology faculty is also right on target. They can be an invaluable resource for you and your future, even after you graduate. For example, after your first job you may still need a job reference from college for your second job. Remember that your current faculty will someday be your former faculty, and staying in touch with former faculty can be a smart career move on your part.

Your name: Jessica F.

Your age: 30

Your gender: Female

Your primary job title: Survey research specialist

Your current employer: Society for Human Resource Management, Research Department

How long have you been employed in your present position? 15 months

What year did you graduate with your bachelor's degree in psychology? 2000

Describe your major job duties and responsibilities. Produce and manage quantitative and qualitative research on human resources topics. Design survey instruments and program online surveys for fielding. Involved in all aspects of data management including the data collection process and performing data quality control. Design the analysis plan and conduct the analysis using SPSS statistical software. Produce written technical reports.

What elements of your undergraduate training in psychology do you use in your work? Coursework in social psychology research methods—learned and applied the fundamentals of survey research methodology, writing technical research reports, running analyses in SPSS, and conducting background research through literature reviews. I also use the information acquired from my statistics course in my job. Coursework in organizational behavior and industrial/organizational psychology (e.g., dealing with conflict resolution, change management, motivation, personality tests) that are relevant in the human resource profession. Volunteer work as a research assistant in the department of psychology. Spent a year coding data on an emotional experiences study.

What do you like most about your job? Meaningfulness of the research—produce research that [human resources] professionals and other customers can use and apply in their organizations to improve workforce dynamics and make strategic business decisions. Other things that I like about my job include variety of work, managing research projects from beginning to end, the ability to work independently and autonomously.

What do you like least about your job? It can be very tedious at times (e.g., data entry, data cleaning, writing) because a high level of accuracy is necessary. The environment is also very structured (e.g., specific procedures and protocols to follow); however, this can vary from job to job.

Beyond your bachelor's degree, what additional education and/or specialized training have you received? I took several classes through SPSS—survey methodology, survey analysis, statistical analysis, syntax, and intermediate topics in SPSS. To design/program Web-based surveys—experience in HTML, Dreamweaver, ColdFusion, and Microsoft Access. I took classes in most of these areas; however, I picked up most of my experience on the job. I have also taken various human resources workshops/seminars to stay current with human resources and broaden my knowledge base.

What is the compensation package for an entry-level position in your occupation? A research assistant position in a nonprofit organization in the Washington, DC, area: $22,000 to $26,000.

What benefits (e.g., health insurance, pension) are typically available for someone in your profession? Medical, dental and vision insurance, 401(k), flexible work schedules (e.g., telecommuting, compressed workweek), tuition assistance, professional development opportunities, and casual dress.

What are the key skills necessary for you to succeed in your career? Ability to pick things up quickly (e.g., learning programming skills, learn about a new topic), strong oral and communication skills, research skills, analytical and problem-solving skills, attention to detail, and computer skills. I have been fortunate to progress as far as I have in research in the nonprofit sector with a bachelor's degree; however, I do think that at some point in time I will need to get a master's or a doctorate degree.

Thinking back to your undergraduate career, what courses would you recommend that you believe are key to success in your type of career? Statistics, psychology research methodology class, industrial/organizational psychology, and organizational behavior.

Thinking back to your undergraduate career, can you think of outside of class activities (e.g., research assistantships, internships, Psi Chi) that were key to success in your type of career? I believe that my research assistantship helped me to get my first professional research position. It made a difference to have real-world research experience outside of the classroom.

As an undergraduate, do you wish you had done anything differently? If so, what? I wish that I would have joined Psi Chi so that I would have been more active in psychology. I think that it would have helped me to learn more about the field and take advantage of opportunities (e.g., publishing research, presenting, serving on committees).

What advice would you give to someone who was thinking about entering the field you are in? A bachelor's degree in psychology provides the fundamentals to be successful in just about any line of work. I think that it's important to try out different types of jobs to see what is a good fit before making a decision to go back to school. A master's or doctorate in psychology is not always necessary, and it really depends on what you want to do in the long run. I started out as a research assistant and worked hard and proved that I was capable of doing more. I was promoted twice within about 3 years.

In thinking about your current career, which of the following categories would you place your career in? Conventional

In thinking about you and the way you prefer to interact with the world, which of the following categories would you place yourself in? Enterprising

Jessica is similar to Kathy in that she is active in the design and analysis of survey data, and she also mentions the use of SPSS. Jessica also highlights some of the additional coursework she completed after her bachelor's degree, including multiple courses in various computer applications. Even though Jessica has been highly successful with a bachelor's degree in psychology, she acknowledges that at some point she may need additional education to pursue the career she wants. She emphasizes the importance of her research assistant position as an undergraduate, in that she obtained some outside-of-the-classroom real-world experience. Jessica is someone who has worked hard and had that hard work pay off. Trying out different careers and working hard in all of them is good advice.

REALISTIC

Making a Real Difference in People's Lives

Your name: Linda G.

Your age: 45

Your primary job title: Vice president of ICF/MR [intermediate care facility for the mentally retarded] services

Your current employer: Handicapped Development Center

How long have you been employed in your present position? 5 years

What year did you graduate with your bachelor's degree in psychology? 1984

Describe your major job duties and responsibilities. Oversee operations of a 54-bed ICF/MR. Ensure compliance with state and federal regulations. Ensure consistent quality services are delivered to residents.

Question to Think About: Have you had any research experience outside the classroom? How might that help you in your career?

Ensure the health and safety of residents and staff are maintained at all times.

What elements of your undergraduate training in psychology do you use in your work? Behavior modification principles. Some things from abnormal and developmental psychology classes. Elements of social psychology.

What do you like most about your job? Knowing that what I do makes a difference in the lives of the people who live here and to a certain extent those who work here.

What do you like least about your job? Whiny, high-maintenance staff and having to deal with society's failure to value the lives of the people we serve. People who don't have a clue what we do passing legislation that affects the lives of people with disabilities, especially those who function in the severe/profound level.

Beyond your bachelor's degree, what additional education and/or specialized training have you received? Nonviolent crisis intervention and several different management/supervisory training [classes].

What is the compensation package for an entry-level position in your occupation? $30,000/year, case manager level, college degree.

What benefits (e.g., health insurance, pension) are typically available for someone in your profession? Health insurance, employer-paid retirement account, disability, and life and dental insurance. Paid vacation time, sick time, personal time, and holiday pay.

What are the key skills necessary for you to succeed in your career? Organizational skills, good communication (written and verbal), creative, being able to handle stressful situations in a calm and professional manner; you have to be able to accept people as they are and not think you can fix or cure them.

Thinking back to your undergraduate career, what courses would you recommend that you believe are key to success in your type of career? Behavior modification and courses dealing with the use of psychotropic medications in conjunction with behavior modification.

Thinking back to your undergraduate career, can you think of outside of class activities (e.g., research assistantships, internships, Psi Chi) that were key to success in your type of career? I honestly never thought I would be working with this population when I graduated. This was on the bottom of my list.

As an undergraduate, do you wish you had done anything differently? If so, what? No. I think a broad spectrum of opportunities is best.

What advice would you give to someone who was thinking about entering the field you are in? If money is a driving factor, don't work the nonprofit sector. Be open to all vocational areas. Be willing to start at the bottom and work your way up. You [get] invaluable experience on the way up.

Question to Think About: As an undergraduate, what can you do to prepare for a career when you have no idea what you may end up doing?

If you were choosing a career and occupation all over again, what (if any-thing) would you do differently? I might consider going into the corporate world.

In thinking about your current career, which of the following categories would you place your career in? Realistic

In thinking about you and the way you prefer to interact with the world, which of the following categories would you place yourself in? Social

Linda very bluntly assesses the conditions that exist in providing mental health services to inpatients; her staff has to deal with "society's failure to value the lives of the people [they] serve." She also points out that legislation can sometimes have unintended effects on people with disabilities. Linda offers two valuable pieces of advice for all undergraduate psychology majors: (a) If money is important, don't work in the nonprofit sector and (b) "be willing to start at the bottom and work your way up."

ARTISTIC

Working Well With Others

Your name: Brad B.

Your age: 27

Your gender: Male

The name of your professional association? American Society of Landscape Architects

Your primary job title: Master's of landscape architecture student/intern

Your current employer: Natural Learning Initiative at North Carolina State University

How long have you been employed in your present position? 10 months

What year did you graduate with your bachelor's degree in psychology? 2003

Describe your major job duties and responsibilities. I am attending school to become a licensed landscape architect and am working with the Natural Learning Initiative's design group while in school. Landscape architects design a variety of outdoor spaces, including parks, residential communities and neighborhoods, campuses, urban settings, golf courses, stream restorations, historic landscape restorations, etc. At Natural Learning Initiative, we design and research outdoor learning environments at schools, children museums, zoos, botanical gardens, and so forth.

What elements of your undergraduate training in psychology do you use in your work? I use my understanding of people, how they develop, interact with one another and their environment, and how they perceive their environments.

What do you like most about your job? It allows me to be creative, work with people, observe and design environments, and hopefully affect people's lives.

What do you like least about your job? There is potentially a lot of computer work involved, but generally there is enough variety of tasks [that] it is not a problem.

Beyond your bachelor's degree, what additional education and/or specialized training have you received? Currently working on my master's degree in landscape architecture and will graduate this spring.

What is the compensation package for an entry-level position in your occupation? Currently about $30,000/year as a student and $45,000/year once graduated.

What benefits (e.g., health insurance, pension) are typically available for someone in your profession? Working at the university has very nice benefits, being state run. If I worked at a landscape architecture firm or elsewhere on graduation, I could still expect a nice benefits package with insurance, substantial vacation time, and so forth.

What are the key skills necessary for you to succeed in your career? Be able to work well with others, both coworkers and clients, be creative within the confines of reality (e.g., strength of material, city ordinances, expense/budget), basic math and technology skills/understanding/ability, time management, work well with others.

Thinking back to your undergraduate career, what courses would you recommend that you believe are key to success in your type of career? Plants courses, more people in environments type courses, more computer training.

Thinking back to your undergraduate career, can you think of outside of class activities (e.g., research assistantships, internships, Psi Chi) that were key to success in your type of career? I did some fetal alcohol syndrome research with rats, and that helped me prepare in many ways. Better understanding of the scientific method, writing scientific papers, the hierarchy of education (i.e., professors, grad students, undergrads, etc.).

As an undergraduate, do you wish you had done anything differently? If so, what? In a way, I wish I'd found landscape architecture sooner, but on the other hand I feel like my psychology degree and my experiences between graduation and going back to school are an asset.

What advice would you give to someone who was thinking about entering the field you are in? I would encourage it, but only if they are truly interested. We have a great opportunity to shape the world in which we live, and that is something that I don't take lightly.

In thinking about your current career, which of the following categories would you place your career in? Artistic

In thinking about you and the way you prefer to interact with the world, which of the following categories would you place yourself in? Social

Brad provides an example of someone who is using a bachelor's degree in psychology in an atypical context—working at the design of environments, particularly landscape architecture. Brad also points out that even though the topic of his undergraduate research (fetal alcohol syndrome in rats) is quite different from what he is doing now, those undergraduate experiences were valuable in helping him to develop critical thinking skills that he uses today. Brad provides words of wisdom and hope: "We have a great opportunity to shape the world in which we live."

INVESTIGATIVE

A Passion for Learning and Growing

Your name: Jacquie D.
Your age: 25
Your gender: Female
Your primary job title: Principal research analyst/project director
Your current employer: Idaho Department of Health and Welfare
How long have you been employed in your present position? 3 months
What year did you graduate with your bachelor's degree in psychology? 2005
Describe your major job duties and responsibilities. My primary responsibilities include the following:

- Project planning, management, and evaluation.
- Grant writing and grant management.
- Data system management including data collection efforts, data compilation, data cleaning, data quality control, and analysis dataset creation.
- Developing research methodology and procedures for the statewide perinatal health survey.
- Analyzing data using SAS.
- Publishing reports and factsheets pertaining to perinatal health.

What elements of your undergraduate training in psychology do you use in your work? Many of my job duties pertain to experience I gained as a research assistant in the psychology department and from statistics courses. These elements include research methodology and principles, advanced statistics, using statistical software (SAS) to perform data analysis, writing analytical research reports, and presenting research to a wide variety of audiences.

What do you like most about your job? I like the variety. I'm involved in every aspect of the research project, so my job is always changing.

What do you like least about your job? I dislike the isolation. Depending on what I'm working on, I can spend several days in my office on my computer.

Beyond your bachelor's degree, what additional education and/or specialized training have you received? In regards to education, I began working on a master's degree in instructional and performance technology and have completed two semesters. This degree doesn't pertain to my current job, and I am considering pursuing a master's of health science. Job-specific training includes several SAS courses and health science/perinatal health trainings.

What is the compensation package for an entry-level position in your occupation? I originally began working as a senior research analyst, and the entry-level pay was about $35,000. I was promoted to principal research analyst, and the entry-level pay was about $43,000.

What benefits (e.g., health insurance, pension) are typically available for someone in your profession? I have very good medical, dental, and vision coverage, as well as a state pension package and life insurance. Supplemental retirement and life insurance packages are available.

What are the key skills necessary for you to succeed in your career? Dedication to research, passion for learning and growing, continuing education, exceeding employer expectations.

Thinking back to your undergraduate career, what courses would you recommend that you believe are key to the success in your type of career? Introduction to psychology major, research methodology, introduction to statistics, and advanced statistics.

Thinking back to your undergraduate career, can you think of outside of class activities (e.g., research assistantships, internships, Psi Chi) that were key to success in your type of career? My experience as a psychology major is what landed me my job. Most of my colleagues have master's degrees, but the primary reason that I was hired was because of my research and statistics experience I gained as a research assistant and teaching assistant in the psychology department and because of the advanced statistics and research methods courses that I took. The psychology department at Boise State really does offer a unique experience to undergrads that they wouldn't otherwise get at a larger university. Undergrads have the opportunity to participate in research projects and work directly with faculty. At larger universities, this opportunity is typically reserved for graduate students.

As an undergraduate, do you wish you had done anything differently? If so, what? No, I feel that my undergraduate [experience] was rewarding and that I was actively involved in the psychology department.

What advice would you give to someone who was thinking about entering the field you are in? There are two aspects to my field—health and research. If someone were interested in the research field, I would encourage them to become involved in the psychology department as research assistants and teaching assistants. I would encourage them to present at as many conferences as possible and to be involved in a publication of a journal article.

Question to Think About: What opportunities have you had to get to know a faculty member, whether formally through a research assistantship, field trips, or professional association activities, or informally, through community activities?

If you were choosing a career and occupation all over again, what (if anything) would you do differently? I would have tried to decide earlier on my college major and would possibly have tried to minor in something else such as health.

In thinking about your current career, which of the following categories would you place your career in? Investigative

In thinking about you and the way you prefer to interact with the world, which of the following categories would you place yourself in? Social

Jacquie is one of "my" students, someone I recruited to complete this survey during the research portion of this project (see chapter 11 for how the online surveys were conducted). She contacted me because in her current position she had just been promoted, and she was looking for a psychology graduate to fill the position she had just vacated. Jacquie was able to maximize her time in college, and she participated as a teaching assistant and research assistant and had experiences at conferences. Undergraduate research methods and experimental design courses really can help you gain marketable skills and abilities that are valuable in the real world.

In the next chapter, I provide some general information about job searches and also add some expanded information about three recurrent advice themes that emerged from the interviews: internships, abnormal psychology, and business courses. But advice is not enough to give you the competitive edge against others vying for good jobs with their bachelor's degree in psychology. In chapters 8–10, I present detailed information and examples on finding job information, selling your skills and abilities with an effective resume (and cover letter), and how to succeed in a job interview. Information gleaned from the interviews you have read is invaluable, but you should also use the sources of information provided in these chapters to make the best informed decision you can about your future and your career. Then go make it happen!

Themes and Advice From the Profiles

7

T aken together, the responses from the online interviews provide an interesting series of profiles of career success. Even though the respondents come from divergent fields, are different ages, and differ with respect to experience in the field, the interviews contain some recurring themes. It is important that you be aware of the needs of the workplace, and the interviews in this book provide real examples in psychology graduates' own words. However, career advice can come from many sources; the research literature is also a source of suggestions on how to make yourself workforce ready.

Making Yourself Workforce Ready

Understanding the skills and abilities necessary for success is important for you and your undergraduate institution because "American workers must now be capable of learning new skills and adapting their abilities as jobs are redefined and typically expanded by the economic and organizational models of the times" (Nash & Korte, 1997, p. 79). The importance of workplace skills has been echoed in two recent, major national reports: the Conference Board report on workforce readiness (Casner-Lotto & Barrington, 2006) and the Spellings Report on Higher Education (U.S. Department of Education, 2006). One of the key expectations of today's workforce is adaptability (a point I return to toward the end of this book in discussing the value of the psychology degree in the context of a liberal arts education). This need to be adaptable to changes in the workplace is underscored by the statement that "most people entering the work force today will have three to five careers and eight to ten jobs" (Peterson, 1995, as cited in Goodman, Schlossberg, & Anderson, 2006, p. xiv).

However, college graduates and employers have expressed dissatisfaction with the job competencies of new graduates (Casner-Lotto & Barrington, 2006, Coplin, 2004; U.S. Department of Education, 2006; Wood, 2004), or their *worklife unreadiness* (Levine, 2005). Alumni surveys can be a valuable source of information about the work skills and habits of college graduates. When rating themselves on workplace preparedness, job prospects, and relatedness of their employment to their undergraduate major, psychology alumni rated themselves relatively low on preparedness and relatedness (Borden & Rajecki, 2000). A survey of bachelor's degree–only alumni found that the top-valued skills were (a) interpersonal, (b) oral communication, (c) problem solving, (d) critical thinking, and (e) written communication (Johanson & Fried, 2002).

Career advice is sometimes psychology-major specific and sometimes applies more generally to the entire workforce. The information provided in Exhibit 7.1 summarizes that applicable to the general workforce (National Centre for Vocational Educational Research, 2004).

General Themes From the Online Interviews

As I read the text of the interviews, I identified five reoccurring themes. First, many psychology baccalaureates mentioned that they had double majored, added a minor, or wished that they had double majored. The general thought was that the double major made for a more versatile background, and many respondents frequently mentioned a greater emphasis on business courses as a recommendation. A second theme that was often mentioned was some sort of hands-on experience, most notably an internship, but sometimes a research assistantship or a position as a club officer. Many of these successful graduates made connections outside the classroom and were able to successfully apply their book and class knowledge to the real world. I believe that current students should be alert to both these themes as methods by which they

EXHIBIT 7.1

Necessary Skills for Workplace Know-How

Workplace competencies: Effective workers can productively use
Resources—They know how to allocate time, money, materials, space, and staff.
Interpersonal skills—They can work in teams, teach others, serve customers, lead, negotiate, and work well with people from culturally diverse backgrounds.
Information—They can acquire and evaluate data, organize and maintain files, interpret and communicate, and use computers to process information.
Systems—They understand social, organizational, and technological systems; they can monitor and correct performance; and they can design or improve systems.
Technology—They can select equipment and tools, apply technology to specific tasks, and maintain and troubleshoot equipment.

Foundation skills: Competent workers in the high-performance workplace need
Basic skills—reading, writing, arithmetic and mathematics, and speaking and listening.
Thinking skills—the ability to learn, to reason, to think creatively, to make decisions, and to solve problems.
Personal qualities—individual responsibility, self-esteem and self-management, sociability, and integrity.

Note. Data from National Centre for Vocational Education Research (2004).

can seek opportunities while still undergraduates and make the most of their undergraduate experience.

A third theme was that psychology baccalaureates often mentioned the empathy needed to work in human services fields and that compassion for fellow human beings was essential for success in their workplace. In fact, interviewees mentioned more than once how society viewed mental health facilities as "last resorts" for those whom society does not know how to handle. Related to this was the fourth theme; online interviewees frequently mentioned a real passion for or love of the work they do, and this was often coupled with the advice that you must love what you do because in many of these professions it's not about the money. There does seem to be something profoundly rewarding in helping others, especially when helping those who have difficulty helping themselves. This profound sense of connection and devotion to improving the human condition is a strong motivating factor for these talented individuals to continue on a career path that may not be financially rewarding but that allows them to reap other kinds of riches.

The fifth theme that frequently emerged was that of "no regrets." A couple of the interview questions started off by saying "If you could do anything differently," and this prompt may have lead respondents to think about regrets or lack of regrets (as mentioned in chap. 2, how a question is asked will shape the answer you receive). Even so, I thought the frequency of "I have no regrets" responses was surprising and interesting. Many psychology baccalaureates, I believe, realize that they could make more money or have different career paths if they furthered their education beyond the bachelor's degree. But there was a real sense of pride (and empathy) in serving the populations that they do. More than one respondent mentioned that it's really not a very good idea to spend a lot of time looking backward at a could-have–should-have–would-have scenario. No matter what career path you choose, you will be faced with obstacles and choices. (Earlier, in chap. 1, I presented advice on dealing with the transition from college to career and also on how your undergraduate training ideally serves as a blueprint for lifelong learning and adaptation.)

Expanding on the Themes

Because they were mentioned so often over the course of our exploration of the different Holland (1974) Self-Directed Search categories, I want to summarize commonly mentioned benefits related to the themes: (a) the value of the abnormal psychology course, (b) the importance of an internship, and (c) the value-added benefits of double majoring in psychology and business (or adding a minor in business).

ABNORMAL PSYCHOLOGY

When interviewees were asked about important courses, they frequently mentioned abnormal psychology. This makes sense because many individuals with a bachelor's degree in psychology get their start in the health care field, and many continue on to managerial or supervisory positions over time. So the knowledge foundation provided in abnormal psychology becomes crucial working knowledge for those "in the trenches."

In addition to providing a tangible foundation for those working in health care professions, abnormal psychology tends to be one of those undergraduate courses that captures students' imaginations. Many students are initially attracted to psychology because of a fascination with unusual behavior, such as maladaptiveness, irrationality, unpredictability, rareness, and violation of standards (Seligman, Walker, & Rosenhan, 2001). We are often intrigued by those who are different from us; because adaptive behaviors help us to function in the world, this observation of maladaptive behavior captures our attention. The irrationality that often accompanies abnormal behavior also captures our attention, whether it be delusions or hallucinations or witnessing the disorganized thought patterns of others.

We live in a world in which it is easier to navigate when patterns and rules exist, and consistency allows for predictability. Abnormal behavior by definition is not normal, and so it is not what we expect from other individuals. This lack of predictability adds another layer of interest for many psychology majors. Abnormal behavior also captures our attention because it tends to be rare and unconventional and often attracts interest from others. For instance, many movies have been made about individuals with schizophrenia or dissociative identity disorder (which used to be called multiple personality disorder), even though the prevalence of these disorders is relatively rare. Finally, the violation of standards that often accompanies abnormal behavior gets our attention. Individuals who break the mold or who act against self-interest often violate standards that we expect others to uphold. Abnormal psychology was a recurrent theme in the interviews because it was intriguing and fascinating to alumni while they were in school and important to many of them after graduation because of its connection to mental health care opportunities. On the basis of these interviews, if you haven't taken a course in abnormal psychology as an undergraduate, you should.

INTERNSHIPS

Internships provide an amazing opportunity to experience a realistic job tryout. An internship gives you the chance to apply the concepts you've been learning about in your classes to the real world. Plus, by showing what you've learned, you could be laying the foundation for or perhaps connections to future employment. Completing an internship provides numerous benefits; Exhibit 7.2 summarizes some of them.

An internship provides a connection between the academic world and the work world. If you have an internship experience in an intermediate

---

EXHIBIT 7.2

Internship Benefits

- Practical, on-the-job experience
- Development of professional and personal confidence, responsibility, and maturity
- Understanding of the realities of the work world
- Opportunity to examine a career choice closely and make professional contacts
- Opportunity to test ideas learned in the classroom out in the field
- Opportunity to make contact with potential employers
- Learning about what careers not to pursue
- Development of skills that are difficult to learn or practice in the classroom
- Potential for college credit and/or possible earnings

Note. Data from Landrum and Davis (2007).

care facility that cares for mentally retarded people, and you hate it, it has still been a good experience. It's as important to determine what you don't want to do as it is to figure out what you like to do best. Internships can provide an insight into a future career unlike any other job experience. Bauza (2006) provided additional advice to interns:

- You are responsible for your own career, so set your own goals in addition to those of the company for which you are interning.
- Ask yourself what type of employee you would want working for you if you ran the company, and then set out to be that type of intern (e.g., someone who volunteers, stays late).
- Relish the fact that you are starting with a clean slate. Don't express feelings of entitlement at your internship.
- Show off your work ethic. For example, limit your personal calls at work. When you are at work, really be at work. Connect with people in other parts of the company outside of your internship position.
- Practice your professional networking during your internship. Try to have lunch with the president or chief executive officer of your company. If that isn't possible, take your internship supervisor to lunch. Afterward, say thank you and write a handwritten note (not an e-mail, a real note on paper).
- When you conclude your internship, be sure to thank everyone who helped make it possible, including those in the company and those on your campus. Say thank you and also send a handwritten thank-you card. Taking the extra step to send a thank-you card helps you get noticed and stand out from the crowd.

Regardless of your future career path in psychology (whether you get a good job with your bachelor's degree or pursue graduate education), I recommend that all my students have an internship experience. The lessons learned, as outlined above, are invaluable.

PSYCHOLOGY PLUS BUSINESS (DOUBLE MAJOR OR BUSINESS MINOR)

Business schools educate students for a broad number of jobs and careers that are important in our day-to-day lives. This broad approach is reflected in the types of faculty who often teach in a business school, from diverse fields of study such as accounting, economics, finance, human resources, marketing, math, operations research, psychology, and sociology (Perloff, 1992). This interdisciplinary nature of business schools makes for a natural combination of business and psychology for the undergraduate. Here is one perspective on this combination:

> Business and industry are increasingly turning to a scientific approach to management in the quest for even greater

performance. Psychology, as the scientific study of people's behaviour and mental processes, has a prominent role at the forefront of progressive business practice. Training in psychology will equip the business and human resource managers of tomorrow with a better understanding of how people act, think, reason, and feel, and with knowledge of a diverse range of scientific methods used to investigate issues in organizational and human behaviour. (University of Western Australia, 2007, ¶2)

In thinking about it, what aspect of any job wouldn't be improved with a better understanding of how people act, think, reason, and feel? Psychology is nearly universally suited to helping improve people's lives because it is people centered. So the combination of business and psychology is a natural one. On the basis of the interviews, you might want to think about taking a few business courses, minoring in business, or perhaps even double majoring. Whichever you choose, it seems clear that exploring your options is a good idea.

More Advice From Successfully Employed Psychology Majors

I really believe in the power of the interviews provided in this book because hearing the attitudes and opinions of these successful psychology baccalaureates in their own words is both credible and persuasive. However, I am not the only one who has studied the attitudes of psychology alumni and gleaned helpful advice from them. A while back, Drew Appleby asked a panel of employed psychology baccalaureates to give advice to current students about how to best prepare for the job market. This advice is so important that I present it here (Appleby, 2007):

- Do not wait until you are a senior to think about what you will put on your résumé. Start this process when you are a freshman.
- Do things that will make it easy for people to write strong letters of recommendation for you in the future.
- Do not be a loner. Develop a network of people who can help you learn about and obtain the job you want.
- Try to personalize your education to fit your specific career goals.
- Develop specific career goals as early in your education as possible, and then do everything you can to achieve these goals.
- Do some volunteer work or participate in a practicum, internship, or co-op program to gain experience and to make contacts.
- Develop interpersonal skills. If you are shy, do everything you can to overcome your shyness.

- Develop computer and statistical skills.
- Do not just learn things to pass tests. Learn things so that you can apply that knowledge in the job you want to obtain.
- Learn to become an articulate and persuasive writer and speaker.
- Get involved in extracurricular activities and assume leadership roles in these activities.
- Learn how to deal with stress and how to manage your time.
- Demonstrate to people that you are enthusiastic and motivated by actively seeking opportunities to become involved in activities that will broaden your experience and increase your network of people who can help you to increase your future career possibilities.
- Do not expect a good job to fall into your lap after graduation. Good jobs are a result of hard work, persistence, and planning.
- Realize that the world is full of people who are very different from you and that you must learn to deal successfully with different kinds of people if you are to be successful.

As you read through this advice, you should notice a great deal of overlap between it and the advice given by the psychology baccalaureates interviewed for this book.

PUTTING YOUR OWN CAREER SEARCH INTO ORBIT

Searching for Job Opportunities 8

There is a ton of information available, in print and on the Internet, about searching for job opportunities and cover letter, résumé, and interview preparation. What I've tried to do in these three chapters is to distill the most helpful information into consumable "chunks." When you are ready to create your résumé, for example, you'll not have the time (nor, I suspect, the desire) to read 100 books or search 100 Internet sites on the subject. Thus, you should view these materials as launching points; by following the advice here you'll have a solid start in finding a good job with your bachelor's degree in psychology.

Bolles's *What Color Is Your Parachute? 2009* is a wonderful compendium of advice for job seekers and career changers. He summarized 16 classes or categories of job-hunting methods:

- Mailing out résumés
- Answering local newspaper want ads
- Using the state or federal unemployment service
- Using a private employment agency
- Using the Internet (posting your résumé, searching employer Web sites or job-centered Web sites)
- Asking friends, family, or folks in your community for job leads
- Contacting a former professor or teacher at schools you attended for job leads

- Knocking on doors of potential employers
- Using the Yellow Pages of the phone book
- Joining a job club
- Conducting a job inventory of your own transferable skills to explain in detail your desired job
- Finding places where employers pick up workers for daily work
- Completing a civil service exam
- Finding ads in professional journals or industry magazines
- Using the services of a temp agency
- Volunteering to work for free for a short time.

As you can see, you can take multiple approaches as you begin your own job-hunting process.

When researchers study the effectiveness of job hunting methods, job hunters do better and search longer when they use more than one approach (Bolles, 2009). In fact, researchers have found that using four of the approaches in the preceding list appears to be optimum. This makes good sense because you would not want to put all your eggs in one basket. Even using multiple methods of job hunting, jobs are not always easy to find. Of the available jobs on a given day, 80% are not advertised or published (Jackson, 2004). This emphasizes once again the importance of networking and developing the ability to tap into this hidden job market.

General Job-Hunting Advice

It's interesting to examine the typical ways in which employers fill vacancies, and contrast those methods with the typical ways that job hunters prefer to find work. According to Bolles (2009), these processes are usually polar opposites. See Exhibit 8.1 for preferred employer hiring strategies and their implication for the savvy job hunter—you! These strategies are listed in order of preference (i.e., 1 is the most preferred method, 2 is the second most preferred method, etc.). The second column includes tips that can help you take advantage of this information.

Looking at the research conducted about job-hunting strategies, Bolles (2009) summarized the relative effectiveness of different techniques. Below I present the five best ways to look for a job:

- Doing a life-changing job hunt. This a three-part process in which you do homework on yourself before you begin job seeking (Bolles, 2009). First, you complete an inventory of the skills you most enjoy using to help you get a clearer picture of what you want to do. Next, you determine the environment in which you are at your best, which helps you narrow the options of where you want to work.

EXHIBIT 8.1

Preferred Employer Strategies for Filling a Vacancy and Advice for Job Hunters

Employer strategy	Advice for job hunters
1. Hiring or promoting from within the company you currently work for.	You may want to get hired at a lower level, or even as a temporary employee, to have the best chance at promotion from within.
2. Asking colleagues for recommendations from within the company.	Make sure you stay connected to your professional colleagues, and ask for an introduction to the person who has the power to hire.
3. Asking colleagues for referrals about people they know outside the company for which you currently work.	Again, make sure you stay connected to your professional colleagues, and let others you trust know that you are looking for a new job and that it would be okay if that new job was outside the company.
4. During a job hunter–initiated interview, the job hunter can provide proof of skills and abilities.	Be prepared during an interview to show what you know. Bring a portfolio of your accomplishments, something tangible that you can show to the interviewer.
5. Use a friend or business colleague for a direct introduction to current job seekers.	It is important to maintain professional relationships and networking; you may not realize its importance until you need the connections the most. Sometimes employers struggle to find just the right employee.
6. Using a job agency to list a vacancy.	Be prepared with the typical preparation for job hunting—résumé, interview skills, and so forth.
7. Placing an ad in a newspaper or on the Internet	Be sure to check this resource on a regular basis; however, note that on the employer-preferred list, this is a relatively low choice that may not have the best chance of success.
8. Reading résumés to determine an interview order.	Make sure that your résumé is current and up to date. Like checking newspaper ads, this employer approach is relatively low on the list; relying on your résumé alone may not be a successful strategy.

Third, you choose a strategy for getting to where you want to go. A systematic search will help you look before you leap.

■ In a job club, using the Yellow Pages to identify fields of interest locally and then calling employers. A job club is essentially a group of job seekers who band together to pool resources and also to provide moral support. The Yellow Pages can help you identify fields of interest that are available to you locally, and with that information you can call employers or visit them in person. But remember to ask whether they are hiring.

■ On your own, using the Yellow Pages to identify fields of interest and calling employers. By calling locally, you have the chance to contact, by phone or in person, local employers. This method is similar to the one above, except that you are on your own.

- Knocking on the doors of the employers that interest you. You use this strategy not knowing whether the employer has an opening or not. This approach is labor intensive, but then again, all of the most successful job search strategies are labor intensive. By going face to face with potential employers, your chances of finding a job are seven times better than if you just send out your résumé (Bolles, 2009).

- Asking for job leads from family, friends, community, career center staff, and former teachers and professors. A job lead is simply a tip to follow up on—a form of networking, if you will. Essentially, you ask anyone who knows you and knows what you can do this question: "Do you know of any jobs at the place where you work or elsewhere?" (Bolles, 2009, p. 35). Let the word go out that you are looking for a job, and when you receive a tip, express your thanks and be sure to follow up on it. You never know where that lead might take you.

If you need a nudge to get you started with any of these strategies, don't forget about the folks in your campus career center. You likely have experts on your campus whose full-time job is to help students like you get a job. These individuals can often help with professional contacts and networking, résumé and cover letter preparation, mock interviews, and the like. They often organize job fairs on campus and connect prospective employers to graduating students. They may also have access to information about alumni in various careers who have volunteered to make themselves available to job-seeking students for informational interviews and sharing contacts. But don't wait until your senior year in college to use the career center's services. I recommend an initial visit at the beginning of your junior year so that you can be more planful about your transition from college to career.

Bolles (2009) also summarized the five worst ways to hunt for a job:

- Looking for job postings on the Internet. Don't get me wrong, the Internet can be a wonderful tool for assisting in the search process, but overreliance on any one tool will reduce your chances for success. Research has indicated that relying on the Internet alone can be a bad strategy; one reason is that many jobs that are filled were never posted on the Internet in the first place. The one exception to this advice is computer-related jobs (Bolles, 2009). The success rate for finding jobs on the Internet is a bit better for those in computer-related professions (e.g., information technology, engineering).

- Mailing out résumés to employers at random. Relying solely on this method tends to be ineffective. Some job seekers will have success in putting all their eggs in this basket, but not many. Some studies have estimated that there may be as many as 40 million résumés available on the Internet—40 million! Using this technique alone sounds a bit like searching for a needle in a haystack.

- Answering ads in professional or trade journals. This method does not have a very high success rate in helping people find jobs, and like the other "worst" ways to job hunt, this method should never be relied on alone.
- Answering local newspaper ads. Although the odds of success with this search strategy vary, overall your chances of success are still pretty low if you rely on this approach alone. The higher the salary sought, the worse answering local newspaper ads works for job seekers (Bolles, 2009).
- Going to private employment agencies or search firms. This technique is another for which you do not want to put all your eggs in one basket. There is one twist on this, however; when this technique does work, it tends to work better for women than for men.

I hope the pros and cons of these strategies are clear by now, but it's worth restating: Use multiple methods in your job search, and try to select the most effective methods. The optimum number of job search approaches is four, as noted earlier; more than that may not yield a good return on your investment. Using multiple methods of job hunting will provide you with the most options.

Best Use of the Internet

According to Bolles (2009), the best uses of the Internet are for (a) taking tests to help you gain insight into your preferences and skills; (b) researching fields, jobs, and employers that interest you (like using the Occupational Information Network, or O*NET, for job descriptions); and (c) making contact with people you know or want to know. The Internet is not particularly good for helping you find job postings or vacancies posted by employers or as a place for you (and others) to post your résumé. However, if you do use the Internet in this manner, listed below are some of the most recognized sites in the job search process.

- Monster (http://www.monster.com)
- CareerBuilder (http://www.careerbuilder.com)
- Yahoo! HotJobs (http://hotjobs.yahoo.com)
- FlipDog (http://www.flipdog.com)
- Job search site, the Riley Guide (http://www.rileyguide.com)

The Internet is an effective way to broadcast your work credentials, but it's been found to not be overly effective (Jackson, 2004), and there are real concerns about identity theft. To help job seekers make the most of the Internet, Jackson (2004) recommended these strategies: (a) Start with a specific job target; (b) identify parts of the country in which you would actually live and work; (c) obtain a list of all the potential employers in each location (the Internet can be quite good at helping with this type of task); (d) investigate potential employers to find out which organizations interest you; and (e) make personal contact before you send a cover letter or résumé. Note that many of these sites offer advice and other assistance, but be mindful of fees and of protecting your identity.

Making Contact: Crafting the Cover Letter

Often (but not always), your initial contact with a prospective employer will be through a cover letter designed to introduce you and accompanied by your presentation résumé. The cover letter is a great chance for you to go into more detail or to highlight an accomplishment from your résumé, or perhaps explain a situation not addressed in the résumé. However, a résumé that arrives without a cover letter sends a red flag to future employers: If an applicant can't take the time to include a personalized cover letter, then just how much does he or she really want this job (Washington, 2000)?

Your cover letter should only be one page in length (Yate, 1992). Why? First, the people reviewing your cover letter don't have the desire to navigate densely packed verbiage (and they value those who can write succinctly); second, the second page of a cover letter can become detached from the first. There are four basic steps in creating a cover letter: (a) Get the reader's attention with the quality of presentation (paper used, font, layout); (b) generate interest by addressing your cover letter to a specific person rather than "to whom it may concern" and by showing, briefly, that you have done your homework on the organization; (c) turn your interest in employment in the organization into a specific desire to help solve a problem; and (d) turn your desire into action; ask the reader to review your résumé or, better yet, ask for an interview (Yate, 1992).

In selling yourself in a cover letter, there are different profiles or themes you can use to present yourself to professional employers (Yate, 1992). For example, when discussing your personal traits and abilities, you might consider using these words: *drive, motivation, communication skills, chemistry, energy, determination,* and *confidence.* When projecting your professional profile, you may wish to refer to *reliability, honesty* or *integrity, pride, dedication, analytical skills,* and *listening skills.* When describing your achievement profile, try to be specific and cite examples of money saved, time saved, or money earned. Finally, in expressing your business profile, you may wish to note your efficiency in solving problems, your economic approach for getting the most bang for the least buck, your ability to develop policies and procedures, and your history in helping organizations achieve profit and success. However, don't let these profiles become something that you incorporate in every cover letter; use them judiciously and, better yet, with concrete examples. If you can tell a story about a past achievement connecting to these profiles and key traits, you'll be more memorable and more likely to have future success. Exhibit 8.2 provides this checklist for creating an effective cover letter.

Following is some good advice for organizing your cover letter (Kursmark, 2006). The body of the cover letter should have three parts (which might or might not be three paragraphs, but should definitely organized into three parts): an opening section that is a quick and positive introduction, a middle section that answers the question "why should I hire you?" and a closing section that asks for an interview and promises contact in the near future. Figure 8.1 shows an example cover letter that integrates the cover letter advice provided in this chapter.

Of course, you'll customize your cover letter not only in your own style but also for each job you'll apply for. In the next chapter, we continue the job preparation process by looking at résumé preparation and how you can successfully complete this very important component of the job search process.

EXHIBIT 8.2

What to Include in an Effective Cover Letter

Address your cover letter to a person, not a title.
Tailor your cover letter to the organization, showing you've done your homework.
Show concern for and pride and interest in your profession; demonstrate enthusiasm and passion.
Cut to the chase and be succinct.
Avoid being stuffy; find a balance between being professional and friendly.
Include relevant job information (be specific).
Ask for the next step in the process (interview), without apology or arrogance.

Note. Data from Yate (1992).

FIGURE 8.1

September 4, 2008

Patrick Otte, Vice President
Human Resources
Micron Technology, Inc.
8000 South Federal Way
Boise, ID 83707-0006

Dear Mr. Otte:

If you are looking for a hardworking and dedicated organizational effectiveness specialist (Job Position No. BOI19898), please consider me for the position!

My education and training, as well as my previous work history, qualify me to succeed in your advertised position. I earned a bachelor's degree in psychology and I completed a minor in human relations in the University of Oregon's College of Business. During my undergraduate study, I was fortunate to complete a 1-year internship at Hewlett-Packard. They were so pleased with my performance that I was immediately hired to work for them on graduation. Thus, for the past 3 years I have worked for Hewlett-Packard in their Human Resources division coordinating employee programs that provide the maximum growth for current HP employees, and providing those opportunities in a fiscally responsible and efficient manner. I've followed the development and maturation of Micron for some time now<em>with your explosive growth, it must at times be difficult to satisfy diverse employee needs. I believe I can help you achieve that goal, and more.

I appreciate your serious consideration of my credentials (please see the résumé included with this cover letter). I would very much like to join your winning team, and I will contact you within 1 week to schedule an interview at your convenience.

Sincerely,

Cire Murdnal

Sample cover letter.

Selling Yourself
Preparing the Résumé That Is Right for You

9

A résumé is more than a résumé. What does that mean? There are at least six benefits to writing a high-quality, well-targeted résumé: (a) You will receive more interviews as compared with sending unsolicited résumés; (b) your résumé becomes your calling card and helps people remember you; (c) knowing that you look good on paper (and digitally) helps build your self-confidence; (d) you will be better prepared for interviews; (e) because your résumé emphasizes results, it will guide interviewers and help them focus on your positive experience; and (f) your résumé will help your future employer justify the decision to hire you (Washington, 2000).

But a résumé can mean something different to different folks in the hiring process. Employers love résumés because they provide a quick method of eliminating possible hires. It takes a skilled human resources professional about 8 seconds to scan a résumé (Bolles, 2009). Job hunters tend to be attached to résumés because using them appears to be an easy way to job hunt. You distribute this piece of paper (or electronic document) and then interview offers show up on your doorstep. If you recall the job-hunting advice from the previous chapter, sending out your résumé alone is highly ineffective: "Less than 10 percent of all job hunters or career-changers actually find a job, when they start with their résumé" (Bolles, 2008, p. 59). A résumé is a selection document, not a hiring document (Jackson, 2004).

The importance of the résumé can be summarized succinctly: "The primary purpose of a résumé is to get yourself invited in for an interview" (Bolles, 2008, p. 60). The résumé also confirms to the employer after the interview that you are the right person to fill the employer's vacancy (Fox, 2001). A résumé should be prepared more like a business card than a biography. You should care not only about what is included on the résumé but also how the information is presented. The human resources person will touch the résumé while reading it, so make sure it is presented in a professional manner on good-quality paper. Always send your résumé to an employer in two forms: electronically via e-mail and on paper (unless, of course, your potential employer has been explicit about the method of résumé submission). After an interview, provide the employer with (another) copy of your résumé, to serve as a memory aid to the interviewer (Bolles, 2008).

Different Types of Résumés

The role of the résumé is changing (Jackson, 2004). First, there are increasing digital demands on résumé preparation because of Internet search engines and the use of technology to cull résumé materials. Second, companies tend to narrowly define work opportunities to fill a specific need; companies want to fix a problem rather than develop and invest in human capital. Third, employees want more than just a paycheck; there is increasing value in balancing workload with family time. Given the changing nature of job demands, it may be time for you to completely overhaul your existing résumé, perhaps starting from scratch. The perfect résumé "arranges your skills, capabilities, accomplishments, education, and values in a document that presents you as the perfect person for the job" (Jackson, 2004, p. 11).

There are a variety of résumé formats that you can use. The most commonly used format is the chronological résumé, and it is easy to read and write. It presents your most recent experience first, and helps you demonstrate continuity. The functional résumé emphasizes your skills and abilities, and the chronology is less important. People often use a functional résumé when they are changing fields. The targeted résumé focuses on the future and what you can do for the company to which you are applying. With this type of résumé, you target a specific position in a specific company to achieve a goal or solve a problem. There are also alternative résumés for which a cover letter fills a void. You might select this method if you have a special situation, such as if you are returning from the military or are a homemaker entering or reentering the workforce (Jackson, 2004).

What to Include, What to Exclude

When thinking about what to include on or exclude from a résumé, use this litmus test: Will this item help me to get invited to an interview (Bolles, 2008)?

You want to use your résumé to attract the attention of the interviewer and present yourself in the best possible light. Having said that, there is a level of professionalism that is expected when you are applying for a job and submitting your résumé. Make sure that the phone number you provide has voicemail capability and an appropriate outgoing message; if you are looking for a new job, do not provide your current work number. Similarly, don't provide prospective employers with your current workplace fax number (Bennett, 2005). Don't provide your current workplace e-mail address; you can get a free e-mail address through many different Internet services. Make sure the e-mail address you provide is appropriate (not something like hotdude@gmail.com or sexylady@hotmail.com). In general, don't use the resources of your current employer (computer time, postage, and mailing) to hunt for your next job—doing this signals to future employers what your strategy will be the next time you are job hunting.

In my experience, some students who have returned to school after a while worry about explaining the gap in their chronological résumé when they graduate. These folks are often parents (usually mothers) who stayed at home to raise children. Sometimes a gap occurs because of extended travel or taking time off from work to care for an ill relative. How do you explain these gaps on your résumé? One suggestion is to be forthright and simply list what you did, as in the following examples (Washington, 2000):

- Full-time parent 2001–2007
- Full-time parent and PTA volunteer at Trail Wind Elementary 1999–2006
- Home care provider for terminally ill relative 2005–2007
- Full-time home care provider for terminally ill relative 2003–2004
- Personal travel 1999–2001
- Independent travel 2003–2004
- Home management 2002–2004
- Family management 2002–2004
- Professional development 2001–2006
- Volunteer 2002–2005
- Volunteer with Habitat for Humanity 2002–2006

My advice is to just be honest. Describe what you did and when you did it. If it is a concern to the employer, you'll be asked about it in an interview, and you'll get the chance to explain further. But you'll have gotten an interview! One other thought—and this is tough to remember sometimes when you are in the job market and really need a job—if a company is going to penalize you for a gap in your résumé because you stayed at home to raise a family or took care of an ill relative, is that truly the type of company you want to work for?

What about résumé length? One suggestion is that "the length of your résumé depends on the nature and number of positions you have held during your unique work life" (Bennett, 2005, p. 5). As you review your draft résumé, ask these questions related to length:

1. Is every word used in the résumé both important and necessary?
2. Is there a way to convey the same information in fewer words?
3. Given that a résumé reviewer may spend 8–10 seconds on your résumé, are you using that attention span wisely?
4. Don't use a lot of white space to fill the page.
5. Don't staple pages; either print double sided or clearly label each individual page.

Customizing Your Résumé for the Job You Want

A presentation résumé is designed to be printed. With a presentation résumé, you attend to its look and feel, font and layout, and so forth. I provide some tips for résumé preparation in Exhibit 9.1. A digital résumé loses all of its formatting when it is converted into plain text (Jackson, 2004). You'll want to make sure you are prepared with both versions of your résumé for every job you apply for (see Exhibit 9.2).

Making Sure Your Résumé Is Technology Friendly

For medium- and large-sized employers, the odds are that your résumé will be electronically scanned and entered into a database with other résumés, then sorted by keywords. The employer will have identified keywords to recruiters and screeners looking for matches. Thus, your résumé (and you) will be ranked in comparison with others on these keywords, making this keyword system very important to your job-hunting success. Some database systems rank applicants on the basis of

EXHIBIT 9.1

Résumé Do's and Don'ts

Do

When listing accomplishments, use bullets (in a digital version, change the bullet to a dash [—] or an asterisk [*]).

Be clear and succinct, but also include the required keywords for database tagging.

Emphasize outcomes and achievements, not activities.

Use specific quantities, percentages, or dollar values when they enhance your description of a result.

Put the strongest statements at the top of each section or paragraph.

Include community and volunteer work if it shows something about you that you want to communicate to the employer or if it helps cover an employment gap.

Choose your font style and size carefully. If possible, prepare presentation and digital résumés separately. For a digital résumé, use a 14-point font for readability.

Proofread, proofread, proofread. Then proofread again.

Ensure that keywords and phrases are listed as statements and accomplishments, and list them as close to the top as possible.

Make your job objective statement meaningful and specific.

If you are professionally published in some matter, mention it (and offer to provide materials on request). Mention professional affiliations if appropriate.

Don't

Don't make stuff up!

Don't use résumé templates—they look like templates, and employers who read many résumés will know you used one.

Don't list references or say they are available on request—that is implied.

Don't enclose your résumé in a binder or folder.

Don't include information such as gender, age, height, weight, race, religion, personal health, or other personal or family data.

Don't include a photograph.

Don't include the mailing address of previous employers; city and state will suffice.

Don't include salary information.

Limit the personal pronoun *I*; it is implied.

Don't fax your résumé unless specifically instructed to do so.

Don't use Greek, Latin, scientific, or foreign terms unless you are positive that the employer's tracking and screening system can process them.

Avoid jargon and unnecessary buzzwords; include only relevant keywords for scanning purposes.

Don't include hobbies or social interests unless they are directly related to your ability to perform your job.

Don't count on your spell-checker to find every error.

Don't discuss the reasons you left your previous position.

Don't broadcast your résumé unless you are comfortable with (a) your coworkers and employers seeing it and (b) headhunters using it without your permission.

Don't leave a silly outgoing message on your answering machine. As a corollary, don't have a silly or inappropriate e-mail address listed for potential employers to contact you by.

Note. Data from Bennett (2005) and Jackson (2004).

Résumé Rules for Today

A digital résumé is the main contact mode for 70% of the nation's employers. You must create your résumé with this in mind.

Prepare your résumé in both a paper format and a digital format.

Take the time and invest the energy to create a résumé that will work for you.

The quality of the opportunities offered to you is related to the quality of the résumé you deliver.

Know yourself and what you truly want.

Prepare your résumé with your future in mind, not your past.

Customize each résumé for the individual job you are seeking.

Make sure your résumé makes it to the person who has the decision-making ability.

Be specific in each résumé as to the job objective and summary statements. Do not adopt a one-size-fits-all strategy.

Find a balance between appealing to the human reader of your résumé and including keywords and skill descriptions that will be captured by screening filters.

Note. Data from Jackson (2004).

how many times a keyword is mentioned, and others measure how close the keyword is presented to the top of the page. However, this heavy reliance on technology and keyword matches often doesn't help employers identify talent. Thus, you need to optimize your job-hunting strategies; make personal contact, and use technology to help yourself get noticed and get an interview (Jackson, 2004).

When preparing your digital résumé (or converting your presentation résumé into a digital résumé), try to follow these tips (Jackson, 2004): (a) Don't use shading or underlining; (b) don't use boldface type for emphasis (instead, use all capital letters); (c) don't use italics; (d) don't use tables; (e) use only sans serif fonts, such as Arial; (f) don't use bullets or indenting—use an asterisk (*) or a dash (—) instead; and (g) use a series of dashes (———) to separate sections of your résumé.

There are many good resources available to help you improve your résumé. But take the advice offered in this chapter: Start by customizing and personalizing your own résumé. Seek out the advice of people you trust, and remember, proofreading is essential! The ultimate goal of your résumé is to get an interview—be sure to design your résumé with that ultimate goal in mind.

Nibbles Are Good
Preparing for a Job Interview

10

If everything has followed to plan, you've crafted a cover letter and résumé combination is that getting you noticed. You've marketed yourself successfully on paper (and electronically), and now the employer wants an interview. Congratulations—the employer wants an interview! Oh no, the employer wants an interview! Your work has paid off, and you've been noticed; you have your foot in the door. The interview is your chance to seal the deal. One analogy is that an interview is like dating, where the employer and interviewee are trying to determine whether they want to go steady (Bolles, 2009). You can also think of the interview as a chance for you (the interviewee) to research the employer. The interview is truly a two-way street: You are being interviewed by the employer, but at the same time you are interviewing the employer. Think of it as data collection (Bolles, 2009). Is this the kind of place where you want to work? Can you see yourself being successful here? These are the types of questions you need to be thinking about during (and after) an interview.

You are more likely to be hired if during an interview you talk half the time and the interviewer talks half the time (Bolles, 2009). If either you or the interviewer dominates the interview, your prospects of being hired may decline. Job interview researchers also tell us that your likelihood of being hired increases if your responses to questions are at least

20 seconds long but no longer than 2 minutes (Bolles, 2009). Try to show the interviewer that you are part of the solution that the company needs and that you won't become a problem to solve (see below for more on this). Also, you are more likely to get hired if you send a thank-you note after an interview, but two thank-you notes is even better—one sent via e-mail to demonstrate promptness and another, handwritten on good-quality paper via U.S. Mail to demonstrate a personal touch (Bolles, 2009).

Here are some other tips on the interview process (Fox, 2001): Don't ask for directions. With the advent of global positioning systems and the availability of Mapquest via the Internet, all you need from the prospective employer is an address, and you can do the rest. Don't make more work for the employer, and demonstrate your ability to handle details. When you arrive, don't treat the receptionist (or anyone, for that matter) as someone who is beneath you; in fact, these support staff personnel can be more helpful and influential than you know. Do not disparage your past employer during the interview (or at any other time)—don't be negative. Exhibit 10.1 provides some additional general interviewing tips (U.S. Department of Labor, 1991).

Doing Your Homework

Even after doing all of your homework, eventually you will have to help the employer answer the question "Why should the company hire this

---

EXHIBIT 10.1

General Interviewing Tips

Dress for the interview and the job; don't overdress, and don't look too informal.
Always go to the interview alone.
Find common ground with the employer and, if possible, with the interviewer.
Express your interest in the job and the company on the basis of the homework you did before the interview.
Allow the interviewer to direct the conversation.
Answer questions in a clear and positive manner.
Speak positively of former employers or colleagues, no matter what.
Let the employer lead the conversation toward salary and benefits; try not to focus your interest on these issues (at least not during the initial interview).
When discussing salary, be flexible.
If the employer doesn't offer you a job or say when you'll hear about their decision, ask when you can call to follow up.
Be sure to follow up at the appropriate time.
Thank the employer for the interview, and follow up with a thank-you note.

Note. Adapted from *Tips for Finding the Right Job* (pp. 19–20), by the U.S. Department of Labor, 1991, Washington, DC: U.S. Department of Labor. In the public domain.

person?" (Fox, 2001). Actually, the employer has many levels of fear. Note that the more of these fears you alleviate (with your cover letter, résumé, and interview), the more likely you may be to get the job offer.

Although the job search process can be stressful for the job seeker, it can also be stressful for the employer. For example, an employer might hire you but not really know if you have the skills and abilities to be successful at the job. How will the employer know that you'll work hard every day, call in sick rarely, and you won't leave them hanging by quitting on short notice? A potential employer may also worry that you might not fit in with the existing employees, disrupting good working relationships. From the job interview process alone, your employer may have to guess at whether you'll do the bare minimum to keep your job, or truly grow and flourish. If by hiring you, the employer makes a mistake, then the employer has to start all over again with the job search process, not only losing resources due to turnover, retraining, loss of productivity, and/or severance pay, but also because they will have these same fears about the next employee to be hired (Bolles, 2009). So while you have a lot at stake during your job search, employers do too.

It would be pretty scary to have all of this on the line with every new hire. But now think about it from the employee's (your) perspective, and do everything you can to assure your prospective employer that these things won't happen. Part of this assurance should come through your work history and work ethic, but if you are hired and work hard to prove yourself every day, then these employer fears about you (and every other employee) will be allayed over time.

Types of Questions You May Be Asked

These are five basic questions that employers are truly interested in knowing the answers to, even if they do not directly ask them (Bolles, 2009): (a) Why are you here? (b) What can you do for us? (c) What kind of person are you? (d) What distinguishes you from the umpteen other people who can perform the same tasks? (e) Can I afford you?

Below is a sampling of the type of questions that interviewees may be asked. It's a good idea to think about your answers to these questions and do a mock interview with someone. Have your practice interviewer ask you some surprise questions. Often, the answers you come up with on the fly can impress a potential employer with how you handle yourself in high-pressure situations, such as a job interview. Some of these questions come from CollegeGrad (2001).

- What do you hope to be doing 5 or 10 years from now?
- What made you apply for this particular job with us?

- How would you describe yourself?
- How has your education prepared you for your career?
- What are your strengths and weaknesses?
- What do you see that you can offer to us, and what can we offer to you?
- What are the two or three accomplishments in your life that have given you the greatest satisfaction? Explain.
- Tell me about yourself.
- Do you work well under pressure and in stressful situations?
- What did you learn as an undergraduate that you think will be helpful in this job?
- Have you ever been in any supervisory or leadership roles?
- What types of activities and extracurricular interests do you have? What do you like to do in your spare time?
- Why should I hire you?
- If you don't mind telling me, what other jobs are you applying for?
- Tell me something I should know about you.
- Is there anything else we should know about you?

Examples of Questions You May Want to Ask

By the time you come away from the interview, you should have the answers to five basic questions (Bolles, 2009): (a) What does this job involve? (b) What are the skills a top employee in this job would have to have? (c) Are these the kind of people I want to work with? (d) If I want this job, and they want me to want this job, is there something unique about me that makes me different from the other applicants? (e) Can I persuade them to hire me at the salary I need/want?

I include next some sample questions from two lists of possible questions to ask in an interview (DeLuca, 1997; Fox, 2001). Note that you may already know some of the answers to these questions—that's OK. The quality of the questions that you ask sends a signal to the interviewer. (Note, though, if the interviewer answers a question incorrectly, do not correct him or her.)

- Can I get a tour of the facility?
- Do you feel I have the characteristics necessary to be hired and to advance in this organization?
- How does the organization regard its employees?
- How does your company make money?
- How long do you think it will take until you make a decision?

- How long has the organization been in existence?
- How long have you worked here?
- How many applicants have applied for this job?
- How many employees does the company have?
- May I have a copy of a current organizational chart, employee handbook, or other relevant publications?
- Was this job posted internally?
- What are the concerns about this position?
- What are you looking for?
- What are your expectations for the job?
- What are your organization's current major challenges?
- What are your strategies to get and keep customers?
- What differentiates your products and company from the competitors?
- What do you feel are the most important aspects of this position?
- What do you like about this organization?
- What does it take for a person to succeed here?
- What is the vision for this company in 3–5 years?
- What is your hiring process?
- What kind of training is available?
- What must your company do to stay successful?
- What were the reasons you went to work here?
- When will you have to make a hiring decision?
- Where are your other locations, if any?
- Who will make the final hiring decision?
- Why have other people failed here?
- Why is your company successful?
- Would this position lead to other job openings?

Finally, make sure to "ask for the order" (Fox, 2001, p. 145). What does that mean? It means ask for the job. About 95% of job applicants don't ask for the job by the end of the cover letter–résumé–interview process (Fox, 2001). Some may not ask because of fear of rejection, because they feel asking is beneath them, or because they don't know how to ask. But you should ask for the order.

What if the interview doesn't pan out? In a recent survey, executives were asked what they think is the most common mistake applicants make during job interviews; their responses included little or no knowledge of the company (44%), unprepared to discuss career plans (23%), limited enthusiasm (16%), lack of eye contact (5%), and unprepared to discuss skills or experience (3%; Lindgren, 2003). Think of each interview as a practice trial for the next opportunity. If you can identify reasons why the interview didn't go well, work on those problems. In some cases, you can contact the interviewer and ask for constructive feedback about the interview process: Was it the way that you handled yourself during the interview, or was it qualifications and experience? Try to reflect on the experience so that you'll do better the next time.

If you've followed the advice in this book (and the many other sources referenced here), these knock-out factors should not apply to you. A successful job search is hard work! Don't take shortcuts; you owe it to yourself to find the best opportunity for success. A wonderful match between employee and employer can enhance your life in so many ways and can make going to work a real joy. A terrible mismatch between employee and employer can be hell for everyone involved. Follow the advice provided here and elsewhere, and strive for the joyful match.

BACKSTAGE PASS: THE STUDY THAT LED TO THIS BOOK | IV

Research Methodology Tipsheet 11

T he responses to the questions that were asked in the 2007 online interview form the heart of this book. I think it's important that you have some background in how these data were collected. Survey researchers time and again have demonstrated that the way in which a question is asked can influence the answer. Thus, by having some understanding of the methodology used, you will be able to place the interviews in the appropriate context.

Development of the Structured Interview

I determined from the start that I wanted to interview psychology baccalaureates about their own personal experiences in successful careers. To do this efficiently, I decided to develop an online interview, essentially, a survey posted on the Internet to help gather information. The bulk of the items were open-ended items, meaning that respondents typed their responses into a box provided. There were also a handful of closed-ended items, that is, items for which respondents checked the correct box or indicated on a scale how much they agreed or disagreed with a declarative statement. I called this an online "interview" because the majority of items were open ended.

Survey research is a delicate balancing act between the researcher's desire for comprehensive information and constructing a survey short enough that it will be completed. Generate too many survey items and respondents will quickly become fatigued, bored, or irritated at the survey's length and self-select out (i.e., quit), and then the researcher does not have the data needed. Make the survey too short, and there may be an adequate response rate, but too few items, and the researcher will not be able to answer the questions of interest. Finding this balance takes some survey research experience and trial and error.

I began developing these survey items in September 2006 and finished in March 2007. The items went through a number of iterations. At this point, I must acknowledge the help of Linda Malnasi McCarter, acquisitions editor in the American Psychological Association's Books Department. She and I traded numerous e-mails and telephone conversations about these items, trying to determine what information would be best for you, the reader. From a pure research standpoint, I wanted to collect as much data as possible on as many people who would complete my survey, but that is not an optimal strategy. It's all about that balance—enough items to get the information you need, but short enough that people will actually take the time to complete the survey.

THE ONLINE SURVEY

Once the decisions were made about what questions to ask, it was time to create an actual survey. I made the choice to collect the data via http://www.surveymonkey.com, a popular site for survey data collection tasks. Once again, Linda McCarter worked with me to finesse any layout problems and to make sure the flow of the survey made sense. The actual survey items and layout appear in Figure 11.1.

PILOT DATA

What appears in Figure 11.1 is the actual survey that was used for the online interviews. To finalize the survey and get some feedback on initial format and layout issues, I asked a select, nonrandom group of Boise State psychology alumni to complete the survey for me. They actually completed the survey as presented except for page 4 of the figure. After evaluating the pilot data, I felt that I did not want to rely solely on qualitative responses, so I added questions about psychology baccalaureates' current job, enthusiasm for the job, whether the job was interesting, career choice, satisfaction with career path, difficulty in finding a job, and satisfaction with income level. As I present different sections of the

FIGURE 11.1

Profiles of Success

Instructions

Thank you for your help with this project. We are interested in compiling a diverse set of profiles of psychology graduates who comprise success stories in psychology. With these profiles, a "profiles" book will be created to highlight those former students who have gone on to success in their chosen field. We are particularly interested in those graduates with a bachelor's degree in psychology who have experienced success in a wide range of disciplines, careers, and jobs. Your generosity in sharing your story will certainly inspire others to attain similar success.

Profile Questions Part 1

* Your name:

Today's date:

Your age:

Your gender:
- ◯ Male
- ◯ Female

The name of your professional association?

* Your primary job title:

Your current employer:

How long have you been employed in your present position?

* What year did you graduate with your bachelor's degree in psychology?

Page 1

The online interview form.

FIGURE 11.1 (*Continued*)

Profiles of Success

Describe your major job duties and responsibilities.

What elements of your undergraduate training in psychology do you use in your work?

Profile Questions Part 2

What do you like most about your job?

What do you like least about your job?

Beyond your bachelor's degree, what additional education and/or specialized training have you received?

What is the compensation package for an entry-level position in your occupation?

What benefits (e.g., health insurance, pension, etc.) are typically available for someone in your profession?

Page 2

The online interview form.

FIGURE 11.1 (*Continued*)

Profiles of Success

What are the key skills necessary for you to succeed in your career?

Thinking back to your undergraduate career, what courses would you recommend that you believe are key to success in your type of career?

Thinking back to your undergraduate career, can you think of outside of class activities (e.g., research assistantships, internships, Psi Chi, etc.) that were key to success in your type of career?

Profile Questions Part 3 (almost done!)

As an undergraduate, do you wish you had done anything differently? If so, what?

What advice would you give to someone who was thinking about entering the field you are in?

If you were choosing a career and occupation all over again, what (if anything) would you do differently?

Page 3

The online interview form.

FIGURE 11.1 (*Continued*)

Profiles of Success

For the following, indicate the extent to which you disagree or agree with each statement.

	Strongly Disagree	Moderately Disagree	Neutral	Moderately Agree	Strongly Agree
My current job is related to my major field of study in college.	O	O	O	O	O
Most days I am enthusiastic about my work.	O	O	O	O	O
My job is pretty interesting.	O	O	O	O	O
My career choice had already been made by the time I finished college.	O	O	O	O	O
I am satisfied with my career path.	O	O	O	O	O
It was difficult for me to find my current job.	O	O	O	O	O
I am satisfied with the income from my job.	O	O	O	O	O

Last Items

For the following two items concerning occupational types, this information should be helpful.

Social (job examples: teacher, counselor, speech therapist, clergy member, social worker, clinical psychologist)
Realistic (job examples: aircraft controller, electrician, carpenter, auto mechanic, surveyor, rancher)
Investigative (job examples: biologist, geologist, anthropologist, chemist, medical technologist, physicist)
Conventional (job examples: banker, financial analyst, tax expert, stenographer, production editor, cost estimator)
Artistic (job examples: musician, writer, decorator, composer, stage director, sculptor)
Enterprising (job examples: manager, salesperson, business executive, buyer, promoter, lawyer)

In thinking about your current career, which of the following categories would you place your career in? (Note: you can only choose one -- sorry!)

O Investigative   O Realistic   O Enterprising   O Social   O Conventional   O Artistic

In thinking about you and the way you prefer to interact with the world, which of the following categories would you place yourself in? (Again, only one choice possible -- sorry!)

O Realistic   O Social   O Conventional   O Enterprising   O Artistic   O Investigative

Page 4

The online interview form.

FIGURE 11.1 (*Continued*)

Profiles of Success

Do you agree to allow the information you have provided, including your name, to appear in the "Profiles" volume as described by Eric Landrum?

○ Yes
○ No

Do you agree to allow the direct quotes you have provided to appear in the "Profiles" volume as described by Eric Landrum?

○ Yes
○ No

Thank you!

Thank you very much for all of your help in completing this online interview. As you know, I hope to highlight the diverse careers that psychology graduates can pursue with their bachelor's degree in psychology. Please know that the time you have taken today will help others. I am grateful for your help.

R. Eric Landrum, Ph.D.
Department of Psychology
Boise State University

elandru@boisestate.edu

Page 5

The online interview form.

data, as organized by Holland (1974) codes (see more below), I also summarize how a particular grouping of careers may include individuals who differ on the quantitative questions.

On the actual survey (but not the pilot survey), I also presented some brief information about the six Holland codes and gave examples of what types of careers are associated with each (you can see precisely what I said on the fourth page of Figure 11.1). I then asked respondents to place their career and then their career preference in one of those six categories.

Even though my pilot survey had a few additions and tweaks before becoming the final online interview, the data from the pilot survey are valuable. Once I started to see actual responses, I knew this qualitative information would be extremely valuable to current psychology majors. Essentially, these are the success stories of individuals with a bachelor's degree in psychology who took the time to share their stories, tips, and suggestions with you. Next, I present two online interviews from the pilot data so that you can be reminded again of the value of psychology baccalaureates' advice in their own words.

Your name: Robert J.
Your age: 59
Your gender: Male
Your primary job title: Vice president, human resources
Your current employer: Simonton Windows, Inc.
How long have you been employed in your present position? 2 months
What year did you graduate with your bachelor's degree in psychology? 1971
Describe your major job duties and responsibilities. Human resources for a $500 million subsidiary of Fortune Brands Inc.

What elements of your undergraduate training in psychology do you use in your work? None that would be for publication.

What do you like most about your job? Key contributor to the success of the company. I have done exclusively done turn-around, merger integration, and initial public offering work for the past 20 years. I enjoy working in midsized companies undergoing change. I have also managed Information Technology, Logistics, Distribution, and Legal at various times. I like diversity.

What do you like least about your job? Travel

Beyond your bachelor's degree, what additional education and/or specialized training have you received? Advanced training in labor relations, organizational development, and executive compensation.

What is the compensation package for an entry-level position in your occupation? Approximately $40K for no experience.

What benefits (e.g., health insurance, pension) are typically available for someone in your profession? Retirement, health care, deferred compensation, stock options and grants, company car.

What are the key skills necessary for you to succeed in your career? Business acumen, systems thinking, results orientation, communications, and an understanding of human behavior and motivation.

Thinking back to your undergraduate career, what courses would you recommend that you believe are key to success in your type of career? Experimental psychology, advanced math, human behavior, statistics.

Thinking back to your undergraduate career, can you think of outside of class activities (e.g., research assistantships, internships, Psi Chi) that were key to success in your type of career? Theater

As an undergraduate, do you wish you had done anything differently? If so, what? Business courses

What advice would you give to someone who was thinking about entering the field you are in? Value integrity, work hard, and understand business from the perspective of the owners, customers, and employees.

If you were choosing a career and occupation all over again, what (if anything) would you do differently? Nothing I can think of, but that is not a line of thinking I pursue.

I find some of Robert's responses fascinating. You can really learn a lot when you ask people what they like about their job, what are the key skills necessary for success, important courses, and advice for success. Here is a second example from the pilot data from a Boise State alumna.

Your name: Courtnee R.
Your age: 29
Your gender: Female
Your primary job title: Special investigator
Your current employer: Florida Farm Bureau Insurance Co.
How long have you been employed in your present position? 3½ years
What year did you graduate with your bachelor's degree in psychology? 2001
Describe your major job duties and responsibilities. I investigate suspicious/questionable and fraudulent claims submitted to my company on behalf of the insured party or claimant party. I handle varying forms of issues that range from auto accidents in which someone is claiming an injury that is questionable in nature or potentially preexisting that they are claiming occurred as a result of the current accident, to home invasions resulting in damage to the property or theft of contents. I also investigate staged auto accident rings, fraudulent or phony billing companies, stolen autos, and catastrophe claims resulting from tornadoes and/or hurricanes. I also conduct extensive background investigations and interviews.

What elements of your undergraduate training in psychology do you use in your work? On a daily basis I am analyzing background data on people, medical documents, police reports, prior interviews, and so forth. Because of the finite and specific nature of the documents and information I am looking at, I have to have concentrated attention to detail. Many of my undergraduate psychology classes at Boise State University emphasized training in this, giving me the skills I now use on a daily basis. Additionally, I conduct many interviews wherein I have to have a thorough understanding of human nature and behavior to obtain the information I need or am trying to uncover.

What do you like most about your job? I love the independence and flexibility my job allows. My manager trusts and expects that I perform my job well and without hand holding. I've earned that privilege over time and now reap the benefits of leaving at noon if I am done for the day.

What do you like least about your job? No one likes insurance companies, so I am constantly working against the mind-set that it's okay to steal a little or lie to an insurance company to get what you need. After all, insurance companies have tons of money, right?

Beyond your bachelor's degree, what additional education and/or specialized training have you received? I have no other degrees besides my BS in psychology. However, I have numerous specialized classes under my belt that I have taken in the course of my previous job and my current one. Before my current position, I worked as a crime scene investigator with a police department. I received extensive specialized training with this position.

What is the compensation package for an entry-level position in your occupation? My company is smaller, so they have great benefits and perks. I drive a company car that comes with free gas (personal or otherwise), insurance, and all maintenance. I have a free cell phone, and an unbelievable 401(k)/health insurance package.

What are the key skills necessary for you to succeed in your career? Being able to work independently is the biggest item. Setting your own schedule, staying on task to get your cases taken care of without needing to be told or checked on. I also work primarily with men, and as a female, I have to have a lot of confidence and gumption to work in my environment.

Thinking back to your undergraduate career, can you think of outside of class activities (e.g., research assistantships, internships, Psi Chi) that were key to success in your type of career? I didn't belong to any clubs in college (although I probably should have). I worked all through college at the Attorney General's Office as a legal assistant/paralegal, and this has aided me so much in my career. So many people hurry up and get out of school in 4 years or less, and don't work or do any outside activities during [school]. If once you graduate, all you have is your degree and no other experience to draw from, you are going to be hard pressed to sell yourself to a potential employer. They want to know that you can carry on a conversation with people outside the classroom and have real-life experience and skills other than sitting in a classroom. I can't stress enough how important—and beneficial—it is to get to know your professors. If you just show up to class and sit in the back of the room, you will just be another name out of hundreds to that professor. Get to know them! Whether you go on to grad school, or start working, you will be required to have letters of recommendation. If no one knows who you are, they can't write anything about you in a letter. Get to know your professors!

As an undergraduate, do you wish you had done anything differently? If so, what? Slept a little more, and tried to get a little better at my math skills.

What advice would you give to someone who was thinking about entering the field you are in? Basically everything I've outlined in the other questions, but be exceptional. Stand out. Make a path for yourself with dedication, smarts, and charisma.

If you were choosing a career and occupation all over again, what (if anything) would you do differently? I'm not sure I would change a thing. My life has been interesting, and filled with adventure and happiness. Maybe taken a few more statistics classes.

Courtnee takes the time to describe some of the intricacies of her position and how her undergraduate experiences positively influenced her. Much of the advice Courtnee offers may also be offered by your psychology faculty members, but it has so much more credibility when it comes from someone who has the same degree and has taken the same undergraduate path as you. Once I saw these (and other) sample responses from the pilot data, I knew this book would have valuable advice for current psychology majors. My next task was to broaden this data collection beyond a pilot sample and to gather more interviews and profiles from a wider and more diverse sample.

Gathering a Sample of Respondents

After the online interview was finalized (long enough to gather important information, but not so long as to inhibit responding) and pilot tested, it was time to collect data from a national sample of respondents. Thus, I "pulled" (survey lingo) a national sample of possible respondents from the National Database of Psychology Alumni (NDPA). Oh, how I wish the last sentence were true! Unfortunately, there is no NDPA. Although the American Psychological Association does a very good job at tracking master's degree and doctoral degree recipients, there is no national mechanism or organization that tracks psychology baccalaureates who do not go on to a graduate education in psychology. This dilemma makes data collection so much more difficult, but at the same time data that are difficult to collect also have high value. Once obtained, they are like gold (or perhaps platinum!) So without the help of the NDPA, how did I do it?

I did it with a lot of help. Essentially, I had a twofold strategy. Recall that in chapter 1, I described how previous researchers had determined that psychology majors who tend to work for organizations tend to have higher satisfaction levels? Well, because there is no master listing of psychology baccalaureates in the workforce, I decided to go the route of contacting professional organizations and asking them for help in identifying members of their organization who were both successful and psychology baccalaureates. So Part 1 of my strategy was to contact the executive directors of associations via e-mail, inform them about the study, and then ask them to identify psychology baccalaureates in their organization, forward materials to them, and ask them to complete the online interview. How did I determine which associations to contact? I purchased access to the Directory of Associations (http://www.marketingsource.com/associations/information.html), an online tool from which you can download contact information for associations and organizations throughout the United States.

The Directory of Associations (2007) has listings for more than 11,000 national associations, more than 16,000 state and regional associations, more than 29,000 association executives, and more than 25,000 contacts with Web site and e-mail addresses. I purchased access to 5,000 associations (including contact information and e-mail addresses for the executive directors). I downloaded this information into Excel files, and I organized my search around the six codes used in Holland's Self-Directed Search (SDS; realistic, investigative, artistic, social, enterprising, and conventional). I did not want to limit the online interviews to only those psychology graduates who were in psychology-related jobs. I wanted to demonstrate that success is possible in a wide variety of careers with a bachelor's degree in psychology, and you have seen from the interview results that this conclusion was appropriate (although you have also seen that at least in this sample, the distribution of people across the six categories is not equal).

So how well did Part 1 of my strategy work? Well, it worked, but not very efficiently. Luckily, I had the help of four enormously hard-working research assistants at Boise State University: Amanda Bailey, Kristin Bowman, Jacqueline Spratt, and Scott Walker. My four research assistants sent a total of 5,000 individual e-mails to executive directors of associations (representing millions of members) listed in the Directory of Associations (Figure 11.2 displays the e-mail template used). From

FIGURE 11.2

(Today's Date)

(Association Director's Name)

(Name of Association)

Dear (Association Director's Name):

    My name is Kristin Bowman, and I am an undergraduate psychology major working with Dr. Eric Landrum, a professor in the Department of Psychology at Boise State University. I am contacting you today to solicit your help with a research project we are working on. In a nutshell, we are interested in highlighting successful individuals from all different types of careers with a bachelor's degree in psychology.

    One of Dr. Landrum's main areas of research interest is to understand the career paths of our students, whether they continue their psychology education in graduate school or enter directly into the workforce. As an undergraduate, you can imagine that I too am keenly interested in my possible future career paths. Unfortunately, little research effort has been given to the study of those with a bachelor's degree who enter the workforce. In my research with Dr. Landrum, we are looking for exemplary individuals who we can highlight who comprise psychology's success stories. I am hoping you will help us achieve this goal.

    We have created an online questionnaire that would take members of your organization no more than 20 minutes to complete. I would ask that you, using your membership directory, identify individuals who indeed possess a bachelor's degree in psychology. Then, I would ask that either (a) you invite them to complete the online questionnaire or (b) you forward their names and email address to me, and I can invite them to participate. The link to the survey is below:

https://www.surveymonkey.com/s.aspx?sm=QxD6uzIxj3gZkLaH3yYylA_3d_3d

Sample e-mail to association directors.

FIGURE 11.2 (Continued)

To help publicize your organization, I will print the name of your organization with each completed questionnaire. If your association directory is not sortable by undergraduate degree, could you please target those individuals whom you believe would be most likely to have a bachelor's degree in psychology? Because of the nature of response rates, I would request as many potential contacts are you are comfortable with, but at least 50 individuals from your membership. Again, you could forward this email to them, or send us email addresses and we'll do the work.

If you have any questions about this project, please feel free to contact Dr. Eric Landrum directly at elandru@boisestate.edu. We hope to be able to highlight, from psychology bachelor's degree recipients, success stories from your organization.

Sincerely,

Kristin Bowman

Sent on behalf of:

R. Eric Landrum, Ph.D.
Professor
Department of Psychology
Boise State University
1910 University Drive
Boise, ID 83725-1715

elandru@boisestate.edu

Sample e-mail to association directors.

these 5,000 emails, about 75 psychology graduates actually completed the online interview. Again, I wished for the nonexistent NDPA. But in worrying about having enough interviews to provide a broad spectrum of careers and experiences, I decided to implement a second recruitment strategy.

Part 2 of the strategy was a more personal appeal. I belong to an Internet Listserv designed for teachers of psychology called PSYCHTEACHER. I posted a request to my colleagues on that Listserv telling them about this project and asking them to send me the names and e-mail addresses of former students who with a bachelor's degree had established successful careers. From this inquiry, I received an additional 15 contacts, to whom

FIGURE 11.3

October 18, 2007

Dear [Colleague's Name]:

My name is Dr. Eric Landrum, and I am a professor in the Department of Psychology at Boise State University. I am contacting you today to solicit your help with a research project – your name was given to me by Dr. XX of XXX XXX University. In a nutshell, I am interested in highlighting successful individuals from all different types of careers with a bachelor's degree in psychology.

One of my main areas of research interest is to understand the career paths of our students, whether they continue their psychology education in graduate school or enter directly into the workforce. Unfortunately, little research effort has been given to the study of those with a bachelor's degree who enter the workforce. I am looking for exemplary individuals who I can highlight who comprise psychology's success stories. I am hoping you will help me achieve this goal.

I've created an online questionnaire that would take you no more than 20 minutes to complete. The link to the survey is below:
https://www.surveymonkey.com/s.aspx?sm=QxD6uzIxj3gZkLaH3yYylA_3d_3d

I would be happy to print the name of your alma mater (under "Association"). The uses of the data you provide are twofold. First, the quantitative data you provide will benefit my undergraduate research assistants who hope to present this data at a regional conference in 2008. Second, you will help me with a book I am writing about profiles of success in psychology. If you have any questions about this project, please feel free to contact me directly at elandru@boisestate.edu. I would like to highlight your psychology success story.

Sincerely,

Eric Landrum

R. Eric Landrum, Ph.D.
Professor
Department of Psychology
Boise State University
1910 University Drive
Boise, ID 83725-1715
elandru@boisestate.edu

E-mail to colleagues soliciting research participants.

I wrote a personal e-mail, mentioning their faculty mentor and then describing the project in detail (a sample e-mail is shown in Figure 11.3).

This approach was labor intensive, but it also increased the overall number of respondents to 90. However, not all the responses appear in this book, for various reasons. I next describe the actual data collection process in a bit more detail.

Actual Data Collection

Before any data collection occurred, I followed the typical procedures for any research study—I obtained approval from my Institutional Review Board. This board is charged with the protection of human participants, and at most universities Institutional Review Board approval is required before beginning the collection of data intended for publication. As you can see from the actual online interview presented in Figure 11.1, the final two questions are pertinent to this. I asked, "Do you agree to allow the information you have provided, including your name, to appear in the 'Profiles' volume as described by Eric Landrum?" and "Do you agree to allow the direct quotes you have provided to appear in the 'Profiles' volume as described by Eric Landrum?" The only online interview responses that appear in this book are ones for which I received a positive response to both of those questions. However, not every interview is included. I also attempted to select a wide range of careers, individuals, and occupations that would provide a diverse set of examples for you to read about and learn from.

Also, you should know that the participants' real names appear in the online interview results that appear in this book. They agreed to have their names published, and I present interviews only for respondents who included a first and last name (although last names are not included in the book for confidentiality reasons). Finally, you should know that the interview responses have only been lightly edited. The content or the message has not been changed, but spelling errors and grammatical mistakes have been corrected. Other than this, these interviews are reported verbatim, that is, in the interviewee's own words.

A Sample Report (Mine)

I close this chapter with a portion of a sample interpretive report based on Holland's (1994) SDS. I completed the SDS in March 2007, and I present in Figure 11.4 the portion most relevant to understanding the Holland codes in actual practice.

I highly recommend that you take the SDS for yourself. You can find it at http://www.self-directed-search.com/index.html. At the time of this writing, it cost $9.95 to complete. Not only will it help you with your own insight and self-reflection about careers and occupations, but it will also help you appreciate the perspectives of the online interviews you have read and the impact of career selection on career satisfaction. The investment in you is well worth it!

FIGURE 11.4

The Self-Directed Search® Interpretive Report

by
Robert C. Reardon, PhD,
and PAR Staff

General Information

Name: Eric Landrum

Client ID: elandru@boisestate.edu

Reference Group: Adult

Test Date: 03/11/2007

Age: 44

Gender: Male

Education: 20 or More

Realistic:	**24**	Social:	**31**
Investigative:	**30**	Enterprising:	**23**
Artistic:	**15**	Conventional:	**17**

Summary Code: SIR

Introduction

To get the most from your Self-Directed Search (SDS) results, read this report carefully. The report answers some of the questions most frequently asked about the SDS; it also provides lists of possible career options for you to consider as you think about your future. The report concludes with suggestions and resources to assist you with your educational and career planning.

FIGURE 11.4 (Continued)

What is the Self-Directed Search (SDS)?

The SDS is a guide to educational and career planning. It was first developed by Dr. John Holland in 1971 and subsequently has been revised three times. The SDS and this Interpretive Report are based on extensive research about how people choose careers. The SDS is the most widely used interest inventory in the world.

What is the SDS Interpretive Report based upon?

The SDS Interpretive Report helps you learn about yourself and your educational and life/career choices. It is based upon the theory that people can be loosely classified into six different groups: Realistic, Investigative, Artistic, Social, Enterprising, and Conventional (RIASEC). Important information about these six types is presented below. Think about yourself as you read about the RIASEC types.

Which types are most like you?

Realistic (R) people like realistic careers such as auto mechanic, aircraft controller, surveyor, electrician, and farmer. The **R** type usually has mechanical and athletic abilities, and likes to work outdoors and with tools and machines.

The **R** type generally likes to work with things more than with people. The **R** type is described as conforming, frank, genuine, hardheaded, honest, humble, materialistic, modest, natural, normal, persistent, practical, shy, and thrifty.

Investigative (I) people like investigative careers such as biologist, chemist, physicist, geologist, anthropologist, laboratory assistant, and medical technician. The **I** type usually has math and science abilities, and likes to work alone and to solve problems.

The **I** type generally likes to explore and understand things or events, rather than persuade others or sell them things. The **I** type is described as analytical, cautious, complex, critical, curious, independent, intellectual, introverted, methodical, modest, pessimistic, precise, rational, and reserved.

Artistic (A) people like artistic careers such as composer, musician, stage director, dancer, interior decorator, actor, and writer. The **A** type usually has artistic skills, enjoys creating original work, and has a good imagination.

The **A** type generally likes to work with creative ideas and self-expression more than routines and rules. The **A** type is described as complicated, disorderly, emotional, expressive, idealistic, imaginative, impractical, impulsive, independent, introspective, intuitive, nonconforming, open, and original.

Social (S) people like social careers such as teacher, speech therapist, religious worker, counselor, clinical psychologist, and nurse. The **S** type usually likes to be around other people, is interested in how people get along, and likes to help other people with their problems.

The **S** type generally likes to help, teach, and counsel people more than engage in mechanical or technical activity. The **S** type is described as convincing, cooperative, friendly, generous, helpful, idealistic, kind, patient, responsible, social, sympathetic, tactful, understanding, and warm.

FIGURE 11.4 (*Continued*)

Enterprising (E) people like enterprising careers such as buyer, sports promoter, television producer, business executive, salesperson, travel agent, supervisor, and manager. The **E** type usually has leadership and public speaking abilities, is interested in money and politics, and likes to influence people.

The **E** type generally likes to persuade or direct others more than work on scientific or complicated topics. The **E** type is described as acquisitive, adventurous, agreeable, ambitious, attention-getting, domineering, energetic, extroverted, impulsive, optimistic, pleasure-seeking, popular, self-confident, and sociable.

Conventional (C) people like conventional careers such as bookkeeper, financial analyst, banker, tax expert, secretary, and radio dispatcher. The **C** type has clerical and math abilities, likes to work indoors and to organize things.

The **C** type generally likes to follow orderly routines and meet clear standards, avoiding work that does not have clear directions. The **C** type is described as conforming, conscientious, careful, efficient, inhibited, obedient, orderly, persistent, practical, thrifty, and unimaginative.

Sometimes the RIASEC letters are used to describe the areas that a person's interests most resemble. For example, we could say that one person is most like a Realistic, or **R**, type. Another person might be more like a Social, or **S**, type. Furthermore, a person often resembles several types, not just one.

How are the six types similar or different?

A six-sided figure--called a hexagon--is used to show the similarities and differences among the six types. Types that are next to one another on the hexagon are most similar. The following hexagon shows the relationships among the six types. For example, Realistic and Investigative types tend to have similar interests, but Realistic and Social types tend to be most different. Conventional types are most closely related to Enterprising and Realistic types, somewhat less similar to Social and Investigative types, but tend to be most different from Artistic types, and so on.

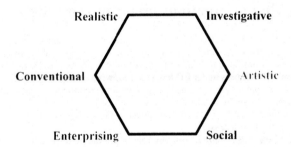

What does my three-letter summary code mean?

Completing the SDS helped you describe what you like--your favorite activities and interests. The three RIASEC types with the highest SDS Summary Scores are your three-letter Holland summary code. Your summary code is a brief way of saying what you like--your combination of interests.

FIGURE 11.4 (*Continued*)

Your interests are mostly a combination of S, I, and R. The first letter of your code shows the type you most closely resemble; the second letter shows the type you next most closely resemble, and so on. The types not in your three-letter code are the types you least closely resemble.

Your summary scores on the SDS were R = 24, I = 30, A = 15, S = 31, E = 23, C = 17. You might think of your interests as a RIASEC pie, with the size of the six slices being equal to the size of your scores on the SDS. The larger the slice, the greater your interest in that area. Score differences of less than 8 points can be considered as similar. Sometimes summary codes have tied scores, which means they are about equally interesting to you.

Can RIASEC letters be used to classify jobs and other things?

Yes. Jobs, occupations, fields of study, and leisure activities can be grouped into RIASEC areas. It is helpful to think of these as environments that are more comfortable, friendly, and beneficial for some Holland types than for others. For example, if you are a Social type, you will probably like a social environment most because social jobs require activities, values, abilities, and self-views that you have or prefer. In general, people who find environments that match their type are likely to be the most satisfied and successful.

What is included in this report?

The SDS Interpretive Report has taken your code and searched lists of 1,309 occupations, over 750 fields of study, and over 700 leisure activities in order to print examples of each for your report.

All combinations of the letters of your Holland summary code were used to build this Interpretive Report. This was done to increase your awareness of potentially satisfying occupations, and to provide you with a better understanding of your future possibilities. Remember, every code is different, and Interpretive Reports vary in the numbers of possibilities printed.

What occupations might interest me?

The SDS Interpretive Report has created a list of occupations based on the letters in your summary code. In the first column, the DOT number printed by each occupation is taken from the *Dictionary of Occupational Titles*, a book with brief descriptions of more than 12,000 occupations.
In the second column, the numbers under ED have the following meaning:
2 means that elementary school training or no special training is required;
3 means that high school is usually needed;
4 means possibly community college or technical education is usually needed;
5 means that college is usually necessary; and
6 means that a college degree is required, with possible additional graduate education.
Occupations also differ in the amount of training needed after a person is hired. In the third column, the + marks are used to show estimates of how much specialized training is needed by a person to excel in the occupation. For example:
+ means 1-6 months;
++ means 6-12 months;
+++ means 1-2 years;
++++ means 2-4 years; and
+++++ means 4-10 years of training are sometimes needed.

FIGURE 11.4 *(Continued)*

Code: **SIR**

Occupation	DOT Number	ED	Training
Doctor, Naturopathic	079.101-014	5	++++
Evaluator (Education)	094.267-010	5	++++
Nurse-Midwife	075.264-014	5	++++
Nurse, Office	075.374-014	5	++++
Podiatrist	079.101-022	5	++++
Corrective Therapist	076.361-010	4	++++
Respiratory Therapist	076.361-014	4	+++
Cardiac Monitor Technician	078.367-010	3	++

What does my code mean?

Some people find it easy to see which types they are like and to find useful possibilities to explore. For example, the three letters of their code may all be next to one another on the hexagon (e.g., SEA); the first letter of their code may have a summary score much higher than the second letter; or the first two code letters are adjacent on the hexagon.

Other people find it difficult to match themselves to any of the RIASEC types, and they feel that their interests are less clear or stable. For example, the letters of their code are separated by less than 8 points, and can be viewed as about the same. They are about equally interested in several areas.

Your interests are a result of what you have learned and experienced up to this point in your life. You may develop new interests related to the RIASEC types by trying out new things. Also, a person's type may become clearer as he or she grows older or has more life experiences.

References

American Psychological Association. (2007). *APA guidelines for the undergraduate psychology major.* Washington, DC: Author. Retrieved October 22, 2008, from http://www.apa.org/ed/psymajor_guideline.pdf

Appleby, D. (1998, August). *Professional planning portfolio for psychology majors.* Indianapolis, IN: Marian College.

Appleby, D. (2000, Spring). Job skills valued by employers who interview psychology majors. *Eye on Psi Chi, 4*(3), 17.

Appleby, D. (2007, October). *Advice from successfully employed psychology majors.* Address presented at Beginnings & Endings: Best Practices for Introducing and Bringing Closure to the Undergraduate Psychology Major conference, Atlanta, GA.

Bauza, M. (2006, July 2). Internships become tryouts for full-time jobs [Careerbuilder]. *Idaho Statesman,* p. 1.

Bennett, S. (2005). *The elements of résumé style.* New York: American Management Association.

Bolles, R. N. (2008). *What color is your parachute? 2008: A practical manual for job-hunters and career-changers.* Berkeley, CA: Ten Speed Press.

Bolles, R. N. (2009). *What color is your parachute? 2009: A practical manual for job-hunters and career-changers.* Berkeley, CA: Ten Speed Press.

Borden, V. M. H., & Rajecki, D. W. (2000). First-year employment outcomes of psychology baccalaureates: Relatedness, preparedness, and prospects. *Teaching of Psychology, 27,* 164–168.

The career path less traveled. (2001, February). *Monitor on Psychology,* p. 32.

Casner-Lotto, J., & Barrington, L. (2006, October). *Are they ready to work? Employers' perspectives on the basic knowledge and applied skills of new entrants to the 21st century U.S. workforce.* New York: The Conference Board, Partnership for 21st Century Skills, Corporate Voices for Working Families, & Society for Human Resource Management. Retrieved October 9, 2006, from http://www.conference-board.org/pdf_free/BED-06-Workforce.pdf

Chen, E. K. Y. (2004). What price liberal arts education? In Siena College (Ed.), *Liberal education and the new economy.* Loudonville, NY: Siena College.

CollegeGrad. (2001). *The simple key to interview success.* Retrieved July 11, 2001, from http://www.collegegrad.com/ezine/20simkey.shtml

Combs, P. (2000). *Major in success: Make college easier, fire up your dreams, and get a very cool job.* Berkeley, CA: Ten Speed Press.

Coplin, B. (2004, September 3). Lost in the life of the mind. *Chronicle of Higher Education.* Retrieved September 3, 2004, from http://chronicle.com/weekly/v51/i02/02b00501.htm

DeGalan, J., & Lambert, S. (2006). *Great jobs for psychology majors* (3rd ed.). New York: McGraw-Hill.

DeLuca, M. J. (1997). *Best answers to the 201 most frequently asked interview questions.* New York: McGraw-Hill.

Directory of Associations. (2007). Scottsdale, AZ: Concept Marketing Group. Retrieved June 25, 2007, from http://www.marketingsource.com/associations/information.html

Driver, M. J. (1988). Careers: A review of personnel and organizational research. In C. L. Cooper & I. Robertson (Eds.), *International review of industrial and organizational psychology.* New York: Wiley.

Farr, M., & Shatkin, L. (2007). *O*NET dictionary of occupational titles* (4th ed.). Indianapolis, IN: JIST.

Fox, J. J. (2001). *Don't send a résumé: And other contrarian rules to help land a great job.* New York: Hyperion.

Gardner, P. (2007). *Moving up or moving out of the company? Factors that influence the promoting or firing of new college hires.* East Lansing: Michigan State University.

Goodman, J., Schlossberg, N. K., & Anderson, M. L. (2006). *Counseling adults in transition: Linking practice with theory* (3rd ed.). New York: Springer.

Hettich, P. (1998). *Learning skills for college and career* (2nd ed.). Pacific Grove, CA: Brooks/Cole.

Hettich, P. I. (2004, April). *From college to corporate culture: You're a freshman again*. Paper presented at the Midwestern Psychological Association meeting, Chicago.

Hettich, P. I., & Helkowski, C. (2005). *Connect college to career*. Belmont, CA: Thomson Wadsworth.

Holton, E. F., III. (1998). Preparing students for life beyond the class-room. In J. N. Gardner & G. Van der Veer (Eds.), *The senior year experience: Facilitating integration, reflection, closure, and transition* (pp. 95–115). San Francisco: Jossey-Bass.

Holland, J. L. (1994). *Self-Directed Search* (SDS) *Form R* (4th ed.). Odessa, FL: Psychological Assessment Resources.

Jackson, T. (2004). *The perfect résumé: Today's ultimate job search tool*. New York: Broadway Books.

Johanson, J. C., & Fried, C. B. (2002). Job training versus graduate school preparation: Are separate educational tracks warranted? *Teaching of Psychology, 29*, 241–243.

Kursmark, L. M. (2006). *Best résumés for college students and new grads*. Indianapolis, IN: JIST Works.

Kuther, T. L., & Morgan, R. D. (2007). *Careers in psychology: Opportunities in a changing world* (2nd ed.). Belmont, CA: Thomson Wadsworth.

Landrum, R. E., & Davis, S. F. (2007). *The psychology major: Career options and strategies for success* (3rd ed.). Upper Saddle River, NJ: Prentice Hall.

Landrum, R. E., & Harrold, R. (2003). What employers want from psychology graduates. *Teaching of Psychology, 30*, 131–133.

Landrum, R. E., Klein, A. L., Horan, M., & Wynn, D. (2008). *Applying to graduate school: Plans of senior-level psychology majors*. Unpublished manuscript.

Levine, M. (2005, February 18). College graduates aren't ready for the real world. *The Chronicle of Higher Education*, B11–B12.

Lindgren, A. (2003, August 11). Research the key to successful inter-views, CEO says [Careerbuilder]. *Idaho Statesman*, p. 2.

Littlepage, G., Perry, S., & Hodge, H. (1990). Career experiences of bachelor's degree recipients: Comparison of psychology and other majors. *Journal of Employment Counseling, 27*, 50–59.

Lunneborg, P. W. (1985). Job satisfaction in different occupational areas among psychology baccalaureates. *Teaching of Psychology, 12*, 21–22.

Lunneborg, P. W., & Wilson, V. M. (1985). Would you major in psychology again? *Teaching of Psychology, 12*, 17–20.

Morgan, B. L., & Korschgen, A. J. (2009). *Majoring in psych? Career options for psychology undergraduates* (4th ed.). Boston: Allyn & Bacon.

Nash, B. E., & Korte, R. C. (1997). Validation of SCANS competencies by a national job analysis study. In H. F. O'Neil Jr. (Ed.), *Workforce readiness: Competencies and assessment* (pp. 77–102). Mahwah, NJ: Erlbaum.

National Centre for Vocational Education Research. (2004). Generic skills for the new economy. In Siena College (Ed.), *Liberal education and the new economy*. Loudonville, NY: Siena College.

Newman, J. H. (1960). *The idea of a university: Defined and Illustrated*. London: Longmans, Green, and Co. (Original work published 1852)

O'Hara, S. (2005). *What can you do with a major in psychology?* Hoboken, NJ: Wiley.

Perloff, R. (1992). The peregrinations of an applied generalist in government, industry, a university psychology department, and a business school. *Professional Psychology: Research and Practice, 23,* 263–268.

Peterson, L. (1995). *Starting out, starting over*. Palo Alto, CA: Davies-Black.

Psychological Assessment Resources. (2001). *Welcome to the self-directed search*. Retrieved July 25, 2004, from http://www.self-directed-search.com/index.html

Rajecki, D. W. (2007). *A job list of one's own: Creating customized career information for psychology majors*. Retrieved December 12, 2007, from http://www.teachpsych.org/otrp/resources/rajecki07.pdf

Reardon, R. C. (n.d.). *The Self-Directed Search® interpretive report*. Retrieved January 16, 2007, from http://www.self-directedsearch.com/sdsreprt.html

Seligman, M. E. P., Walker, E. F., & Rosenhan, D. L. (2001). *Abnormal psychology* (4th ed.). New York: Norton.

Smith, T. W. (2007). *Job satisfaction in the United States* Retrieved December 7, 2007, from http://www-news.uchicago.edu/releases/07/pdf/070417.jobs.pdf

Snyder, T. D., Dillow, S. A., & Hoffman, C. M. (2008). *Digest of education statistics: 2007* (NCES Publication No. 2008-022). Washington, DC: U.S. Government Printing Office.

Sternberg, R. J. (Ed.). (1997). *Career paths in psychology: Where your degree can take you*. Washington, DC: American Psychological Association.

Super, C. M., & Super, D. E. (1995). *Opportunities in psychology careers*. Lincolnwood, IL: VGM Career Horizons.

University of Western Australia. (2007). *A productive partnership: Psychology & business*. Retrieved July 27, 2008, from http://www.psychology.uwa.edu.au/for/prospective_postgraduates/post_graduate_courses

U.S. Department of Education. (2006). *A test of leadership: Charting the future of U.S. higher education*. Washington, DC: Author.

U.S. Department of Labor. (1991). *Tips for finding the right job*. Washington, DC: Author.

Wahlstrom, C., & Williams, B. K. (2004). *College to career: Your road to personal success*. Mason, OH: South-Western.

Washington, T. (2000). *Résumé power: Selling yourself on paper*. Bellevue, WA: Mount Vernon Press.

Wood, F. B. (2004). Preventing postparchment depression: A model of career counseling for college seniors. *Journal of Employment Counseling, 41,* 71–79.

Yancey, G. B., Clarkson, C. P., Baxa, J. D., & Clarkson, R. N. (2003). Examples of good and bad interpersonal skills at work. *Eye on Psi Chi, 7*(3), 40–41.

Yate, M. (1992). *Cover letters that knock 'em dead*. Holbrook, MA: Bob Adams.

Index

About the Author

R. Eric Landrum, PhD, is a professor of psychology at Boise State University (BSU). He received his doctorate in cognitive psychology (with an emphasis in quantitative methodology) from Southern Illinois University–Carbondale in 1989. His research interests center on the study of educational issues, identifying those conditions that best facilitate student success (broadly defined). He has given more than 200 presentations at professional conferences and has published 17 books or book chapters and more than 60 articles in scholarly, peer-reviewed journals. His work has appeared in journals such as *Teaching of Psychology, College Teaching, Educational and Psychological Measurement,* the *Journal of College Student Development,* the *Journal of Research and Development in Education,* and *College Teaching.* Dr. Landrum has worked with more than 200 undergraduate research assistants, and in 17 years at BSU, he has taught more than 10,000 students. During summer 2008, he participated in the National Conference for Undergraduate Education in Psychology at the University of Puget Sound, serving as the leader of a working group concerned with the desired results of an undergraduate education in psychology.

Dr. Landrum is the coeditor and author of two chapters in *Protecting Human Subjects: Departmental Subject Pools and*

Institutional Review Boards (1999, American Psychological Association) and lead author of *The Psychology Major: Career Options and Strategies for Success* (3rd ed., 2007). He is a member of the American Psychological Association and a fellow of the Society for the Teaching of Psychology (American Psychological Association Division 2), and he was recently elected its secretary. In addition, Dr. Landrum is an active member of the Midwestern Psychological Association and the Rocky Mountain Psychological Association. He is an award-winning teacher (Associated Students of BSU Outstanding Faculty Member Award, 1994 and 2005; BSU Foundation Scholars Outstanding Teacher Award, 2002) and researcher (BSU's College of Social Sciences and Public Affairs Tenured Research Award, 2004). At BSU, Dr. Landrum teaches courses in general psychology (in the classroom and online), introduction to the psychology major, statistical methods, research methods, and psychological measurements. He has served as national president of the Council of Teachers of Undergraduate Psychology and has served Psi Chi both locally and regionally. He was department chair from 1996 to 2000 and from 2005 to 2006.